Folded Star

⟨Mitred Patchwork⟩

Frontispiece Back of jacket worked in polyester
and cotton lawn, printed cottons and slubbed voile

Folded Star

⟨Mitred Patchwork⟩

Margaret K. Wright

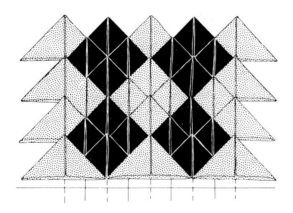

Dover Publications, Inc., New York

Library of Congress Cataloging-in-Publication Data

Wright, Margaret K.
  Folded star.

  (Dover needlework series)
  Bibliography: p.
  Includes index.
  1. Patchwork—Patterns. 2. Quilting—Patterns.
I. Title. II. Series.
TT835.W75   1986   746.46   87-5420
ISBN 0-486-25546-8 (pbk.)

Contents

Acknowledgments

I should like to thank Michael Bull, who kindly photographed all the practical work. I am most grateful to Margaret Willford for helping with the experiments and lending her work, to Harriet Faulkner for patiently reading and correcting the typescript, and to my daughter Carol Davis for working and checking all the instructions.

I also thank Sue Gingell, Janice Hay, June Linsley, Debra Stevens and Barbara Wilson for examples of their work and Anne Heegaard for working part of the Bishop's mitre during her visit to this country. The authorship of work appearing in this book is as follows: Frontispiece, Figs. 33, 37, 41, 53, 58, 59, 61, 67, 72, 75, 95, 107, 108, 127, 128, 130, 131, 132, 136, 142, 144, 147, 149, 151, 156 – the author; Figs. 52, 133 – the author with Anne Heegaard; Fig. 1 – June Linsley; Fig. 29 – Janice Hay; Figs. 60, 65, 70, 94, 111, 140 – Margaret Willford; Fig. 92 – Sue Gingell; Fig. 113 – Debra Stevens; Fig. 139 – Carol Davis; Fig. 155 – Piddington Workshop, and Fig. 158 – Barbara Wilson.

Further thanks go to the many friends who have encouraged me to write this book.

Introduction

In many societies, small scraps of fabrics have been carefully saved and then reused. The best parts of worn or torn saris have produced most beautiful patchwork crib covers; Jacob's coat of many colours was probably made of patches, and one of the earliest extant pieces of needlecraft, a canopy of the tenth century in the Boulak Museum, Cairo, is a patchwork of many patterns in dyed gazelle hide. During the eighteenth and nineteenth centuries the settlers in North America brightened their sombre homes with colourful patchwork bed covers, curtains and cushions.

During this century there has been a revival of interest in patchwork. With the many new fibres, methods of dyeing and printing, construction and finishes of fabrics, the opportunities for experimenting and developing the craft are limitless; and, since patchwork is an economical form of textile craft, there is scope for creative work at a moderate cost. Using colour, pattern and texture there are endless possibilities for ingenuity.

Patchwork has given, and continues to give, pleasure to both the maker and the viewer, as well as enhancing surroundings. As a result of its long, and worldwide history, patchwork has taken many forms: *appliqué*, where patches are sewn down on a background; *pieced work*, where regular shapes are joined together to make a large piece of fabric; *log-cabin*, where fabric strips or ribbon are applied from the centre outwards onto squares which are then joined together; *crazy work*, where irregular shapes are overlapped and applied to cover a backing fabric completely and then elaborated with embroidery; *pillow patches*, where regular shapes are lined and stuffed to make small cushions which are then joined together, and *cathedral windows*, where plain fabric is folded over squares of printed fabric.

The folding of small squares of fabric and applying them to a backing to form interesting patterns and textures appears to be a more recent development, although an American quilt of 1850, recorded in *America's Quilts and Coverlets* by Safford and Bishop, has small pieces of folded triangles of fabrics stitched in concentric circles. These form inset circles of petal-like patches in a quilt called 'Sunburst'. Plain, patterned and gingham fabrics have been used in mainly red, orange, brown, gold and white. Agnes M. Mail, in her book *Patches Old and New*, published in 1937, records a form of petal patchwork 'invented by an ingenious woman' and has a photograph of a handkerchief sachet where the patches form a three-dimensional floral effect. In Dorothea Nield's book *Adventures in Patchwork*, published in 1975, a Spanish skirt made in silk, folded, equilateral triangles can be seen. Bands of small folded triangle patches are incorporated in garments made and worn by the Lisu hill-tribes of Thailand. Edges of garments have often been decorated using folded patches of fabric that form triangles, saw-toothed or prairie point edges.

Folding ribbon, tape or lengths of rouleau to form a mitred point has often been used for decorative edgings, as supporting loops or fastening buttons. Folding rectangular patches to form mitred triangles and applying them to a backing appears to be a development during the second half of this century. It is the folding of a mitre to form a right-angled triangle that distinguishes this recent development, which I call *mitred patchwork*. The mitre gives the applied patches an extra dimension, and the ever-changing kaleidoscope of colours, patterns and textures offers an opportunity for its continuing development. Although the application of the patches can vary a

1 'Somerset Flower Garden' quilt

Guild newsletter. She says that the method was taught to her by a Mrs Midgley from Kent. At the time, Mrs Willesdon was living in Somerset and consequently the editor titled the article 'Patchwork Method from Somerset'. In 1980 the Embroiderers' Guild exhibition included a beautiful mitred patchwork quilt made by Mrs June Linsley and named 'Somerset Flower Garden' (*figure 1*). The exhibition catalogue described the method as *Somerset patchwork* – a shortened version of the title of Anne Willesdon's article – and since then many people have used this name.

In America the name *folded star patchwork* is used but, as so many other patterns can be produced, this would seem a restrictive title. A further adaptation of the method has been published by McCalls in an article for their magazine *Needlework and Crafts*, where the patches are made from circles, folded into mitres and held in place with machining, although the points are still held down by hand stitching. The cutting out of small circles is rather time-consuming compared with rectangles or squares, which can be produced more quickly in quantity. In 1982 the winner of the Craft and Hobby Industry Association's British Craft Award of the Year was the Quiltery's 'Folded Star' Patchwork Cushion Kit. The kit uses the mitred triangle patch applied in concentric circles. Similar kits are being produced in Canada and America for cushions, pictures, sachets, and many small articles. One kit produced in America has a pattern known as *Connie's chicken coop*!

During teaching, mitred patchwork has given me, my pupils and friends, absorbing hours of creative work and produced many enquiries from visitors. Through these enquiries and the general interest aroused I have been encouraged to write this book, and hope that the method will continue to develop and grow in the future.

great deal, the central fold lines of the mitre are constant and give the work its distinctive character.

The earliest recording in Britain that I have found of the method for applying mitred patches in concentric circles was written by Anne Willesdon in 1979 in the first edition of the Quilters'

1 Materials and equipment

FABRICS AND NOTIONS

Fabrics for the patches

As a beginner with this method it is best to use closely-woven cotton fabrics that are plain or have a small pattern, and are of summer-dress weight, as they are the easiest to handle. Examples of these fabrics can vary from printed calico to percale, poplins, lawns, piqué, gingham, organdie, medium-weight sailcloth, cambric and batiste. Fine linens can also be used. Many of these fabrics are made from mixtures or blends of fibres. Cotton and polyester are often used together in what used to be a traditionally all-cotton fabric. You will find that these types of fabrics are perfectly suitable but require care in pressing the folds and handling as they are more springy and resistant to creasing than those made from 100 per cent cotton.

As you become more experienced and ready to experiment, many varied and different fabrics can be used, such as satin, tweed, velvet, organza, crêpe de Chine, denim, flannel, lamé, lace, gros-grain, gaberdine, gloving leather and shantung, to name but a few. They can be made from a wide variety of fibres – cotton, wool, silk, linen, viscose, rayon, acetates or synthetics. The choice of fabric will depend on the use of the article being made and the effect you require in the design.

You must consider if the article is to be washed. If it is, then all fabrics for the article must be washable, and, in the case of materials that might shrink or stretch slightly, they should be washed before being used in the patchwork. If the variety of fabrics used are normally washed at different temperatures, then the final article will need to be washed at the code of the fabric requiring the lowest temperature and mildest washing programme.

For articles that require no specific cleaning method the choice will depend upon the skill you have for handling many types of fabrics. It will also depend on the effect you require in the design and how well the fabric will fold to achieve that effect. Some areas can be made very rich by using satins and velvets. Lovely textures can be incorporated with the use of tweeds. Printed patterned fabrics will give the appearance of texture; because the patches are so small the patterns are not easily seen. Fine stripes can make some very interesting effects, while lamé and crystal organza can be very exotic. Soft gloving leathers can give very subtle textures, colours and soft folds. Another consideration is how much the article will be handled or collect dust. Fabrics can have many different finishes which protect them from dirt penetration: chintz, glazed fabrics, P.V.C. and leather. Cleaning with a soft brush will easily remove surface dust from such fabrics; vacuum cleaning is also very satisfactory.

With knitted fabrics care must be taken to select those varieties that will not ladder, since the cut edges of the patches are not neatened. Many knitted fabrics stretch easily or curl, making them difficult to retain accuracy. When using the standard patch, steam pressing can help, or a piece of Bondaweb placed under the turning eliminates the trouble but makes the turned edge stiffer. Some double-jersey fabrics are very stable and can be used with confidence. When experimenting with three-dimensional work, the stretchability of knitted fabrics can be an advantage in producing effects that woven fabrics cannot achieve.

As you experiment further, become skilled at

manipulating fabrics and find a wider use for the patches, you will discover that any fabrics can be incorporated so long as they are suitable for use, have the right colour and texture, and fold to achieve the desired effect.

The backing fabric

This fabric needs to be closely woven and of light or medium weight. Sheeting, or fine unbleached or bleached calico are suitable. It is always wise to pre-shrink these fabrics. This can be done by thoroughly soaking in hot water and pressing whilst damp. As the backing fabric will be covered with patches, it is not necessary to consider colour and texture.

Always allow a good margin of surplus backing fabric beyond the final size of the motif, especially if you work in a frame.

Thread

A good-quality machine thread is used for the stitching. As the stitches should not be seen, the colour should blend with the colour of the patches. I have found that one blending colour is suitable throughout the patching, occasionally changing for very dark shades or white. Invisible thread can be used if you can control its springiness and securely cast it on and off. Choose the machine thread most suited to the fabric being used. So many fabrics contain more than one fibre that multi-purpose machine threads are especially suitable, and are made in a wide range of colours. If your fabrics are 100 per cent cotton, an all-cotton machine thread is most suitable. Do not use machine embroidery thread as this type is not strong enough. Larger cobs or reels containing 500 or 1000 metres in basic colours are most suitable, as a great deal of thread is used for the patching and a number of 100 metre reels could prove rather costly. To prevent threads knotting they can be run through a piece of beeswax. Surplus wax should be removed by running the thread between the index finger and the thumb nail.

Needles

Use a fine, small-eyed needle; Sharps 7 or 8 are good. If you prefer a shorter needle, a Betweens 7 or 8 can be used. When you start to experiment and use leather, a fine glover's needle is best.

FRAMES

It is not always necessary to use a frame, especially for small pieces of work. The advantages of using a frame are that it leaves both hands free and it is not so tiring to work more difficult fabrics. With both hands free you can hold the patch in place whilst securing stitches are completed.

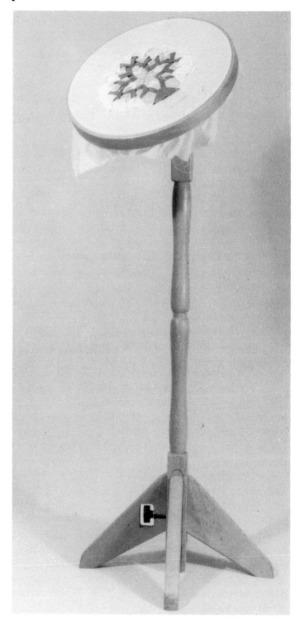

2   Tambour frame on stand

10

A tambour frame

A tambour (round) frame can be used as long as the motif fits well within the inner ring. If the frame is not on a stand (*figure 2*), then support it on a table edge and stabilise with a heavy book (*figure 3*).

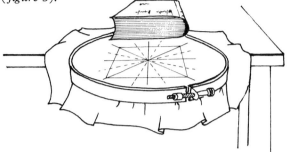

3   Tambour frame supported by a heavy book

Preparing a tambour frame

1   Bind the inner ring with narrow tape taking care to stitch the end in place securely (*figure 4*).
2   Mark the backing fabric (see Chapter 2 on preparation). This will be the right side. Remember to leave a good margin of fabric beyond the markings.
3   Cover the inner ring with the backing fabric right side up.
4   Loosen the screw on the outer ring. Grip the outer ring over the fabric and inner ring.
5   Tighten the screw (*figure 5*).
6   Make the fabric taut by pulling inwards with the grain of the fabric (*figure 6*).

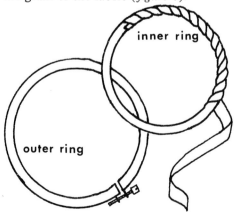

4   Binding the inner ring of a tambour frame to give a better grip

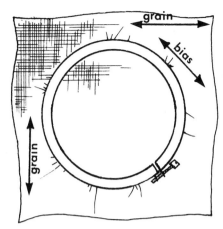

5   Placing the fabric between the two rings of a tambour frame

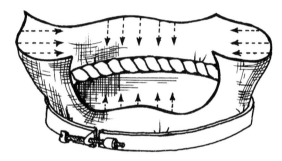

6   Pulling fabric taut in a tambour frame

A slate frame

Slate (rectangular) frames are particularly useful for large pieces of work. An old picture frame is a useful substitute or four slats of wood joined at the corners with simple L-halved joints (*figure 7*). These substitute frames have the marked backing fabric stretched over them and held in place with drawing pins or staples. If not on a stand, a slate

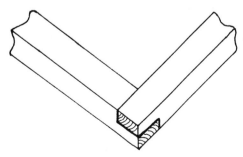

7   L-halved joint for making a simple slate frame

frame can be supported on a table in the same way as the tambour frame or it can be clamped with a small G cramp to give rigidity (*figure 8*).

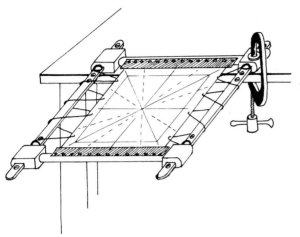

8   A slate frame supported by a G cramp

Dressing a slate frame

1   Mark the backing fabric on the right side and leave a good margin of fabric beyond the markings (see Chapter 2 on preparation). The width of the fabric should not be greater than the tapes on the rollers. Cut the fabric true to the grains.

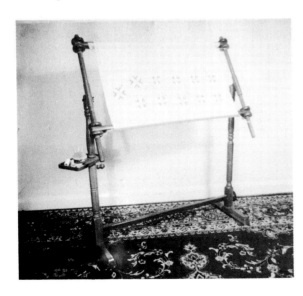

9   Dressed slate frame on floor stand

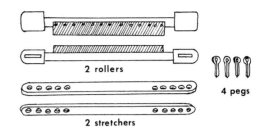

10   Parts of a slate frame

2   Mark the centres of the top and bottom fabric edges and the tapes on the rollers.

3   Turn under and press a 6mm ($\frac{1}{4}$in) turning to the wrong side of the fabric along the top and bottom edges.

4   Enclose a length of string in a small turning along the side edges, using a small running stitch. Take care not to catch the string in the stitches (*figure 11a*).

5   Join the top and bottom edges to the roller tapes by matching the centre markings, having right sides together and oversewing. Always stitch from the centres towards the sides (*figure 11b*).

6   Put the frame stretchers in place, pulling the fabric taut.

7   Lace the side edges of the fabric to the stretchers with string.

8   Pull the lacing strings to tighten the fabric across its width. This is easier with the aid of a

11   Dressing a slate frame

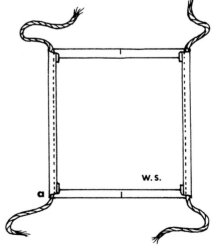

a Preparing the fabric

friend when using a very large frame. Secure all strings by tying to the frame (*figure 11c*).

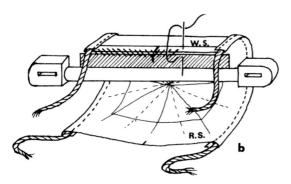

b Oversewing fabric to tape on rollers

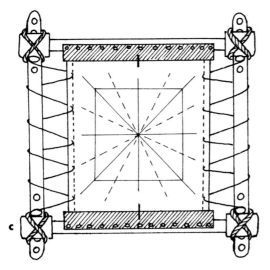

c Completed dressed frame

Dressing a picture frame or home-made frame

1 Mark the right side of the backing fabric leaving a margin beyond the markings (see Chapter 2 on preparation).

2 Starting at the top left-hand corner and keeping the fabric on the straight of grain, pin the top edge in place using drawing pins or a staple gun.

3 Secure the right-hand edge on the grain of the fabric.

4 Starting at the lower left-hand corner, pull the fabric to the same line of grain as the bottom right-hand corner and secure in place. Secure the left-hand edge (*figure 12a*).

5 Secure the lower edge (*figure 12b*).

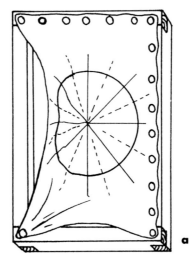

12 Dressing a picture or home-made frame
  a Stretching fabric onto the frame

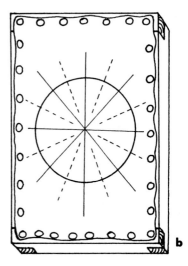

b Completed dressed frame

2 Preparation of fabrics

All markings for the backing fabric should be made with a sharp H pencil or a transferring pen which contains water-soluble colouring that can be removed with a damp cloth. Never press the fabric before removing markings, otherwise they become permanent. Water-soluble markers can be obtained from the haberdashery section in most department stores. An H pencil or tailor's chalk can be used for marking round the templates for patches.

THE BACKING FABRIC

Marking for a square motif

1 In the centre of the fabric mark a 10cm (4in) square. Larger squares can be used, but 10cm (4in) is a convenient size for learning the process.

2 Draw in the diagonal lines. Draw in the central vertical and horizontal lines. Extend all lines beyond the square.

3 Using a broken line, mark the bisecting lines between those already drawn, extending the lines beyond the square (*figure 13*).

Marking for a circle

1 In the centre of the fabric mark a 10cm (4in) diameter circle.

2 Mark eight sections at 45 degrees, extending the lines beyond the circle.

3 Using a broken line, mark the bisecting lines at 22.5 degrees, extending the lines beyond the circle (*figure 14*).

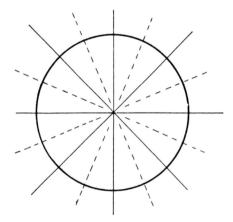

14 Marking the backing fabric for a 10cm (4in) diameter motif

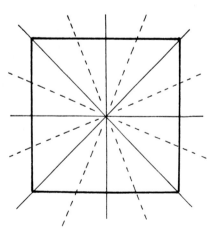

13 Marking the backing fabric for a 10cm (4in) square motif

Marking the seam allowance

A seam allowance must be marked on the backing fabric. Decide if this allowance is to be beyond or inside the circle or square or shape. I have found it useful to mark the seam line with a broken line and the cutting line with a continuous line (*figure 15*).

If you intend to make a number of squares or circles all the same size, cut a cardboard template to size and mark the divisions on the card. This will make transferring very much quicker and is particularly useful for making quilts or sets of similar-sized articles. If you can see through the backing fabric, the markings can be drawn on paper with black ink. The paper is then placed under the fabric and traced. For the variations in chapter 4 and further experiments, you may like to make a cardboard template 15cm (6in) in diameter. For any very large pieces of work, further bisecting lines are necessary. These bisecting lines need not reach to the centre point but should still extend beyond the square or circle (*figure 15a and b*).

Since the distance of the overlapping is usually judged by eye, it is helpful to mark a series of inner rings inside the square or circle so that there is a check on the patches being applied evenly from the centre. Any distance can be made between the inner circles, as they are only to act as guide lines (*figure 15a and b*).

THE PATCHES

For your first attempt select three or four dress-weight woven cotton fabrics that have a pleasing range of tones from light to dark in one colour. The number of patches required for the first practice piece is given with the instructions in Chapter 3. As you progress you will begin to select contrasts, tones and complementary colours to produce many different patterns and effects.

It is time-saving to use mass-production methods of cutting and pressing the patches. You will therefore require some stiff card to make accurate templates. For marking the fabric use a sharp H pencil or a tailor's chalk pencil of a suitable colour that can easily be seen on the fabric.

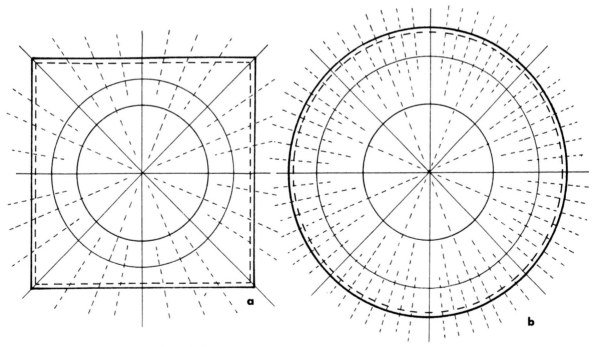

15   Markings for larger motifs include seam
     allowance, additional bisecting lines and guide
     lines
     a Marking a large square   b Marking a large circle

Standard patches

1 Make a template in card measuring 20cm (8in) by 3cm (1¼in). Mark in four equal sections of 5cm (2in). Mark a line 6mm (¼in) parallel to one long edge (*figure 16*).

2 Keeping the long edges of the template accurately on the grain of the fabric, draw round the template. Continue marking along the fabric to form a long strip marked off in 20cm (8in) sections. If the fabric is only long enough to take a final group of three instead of four, always mark the three divisions otherwise the group can easily be mistaken for a group of four and the resulting patches will be too small.

3 Mark a number of strips onto each of your selected fabrics (*figure 17a*).

4 Cut the fabrics into strips along the marked lines.

5 Press a 6mm (¼in) turning to the wrong side along one long edge (*figure 17b*).

6 Cut on marked divisions 20cm (8in) apart.

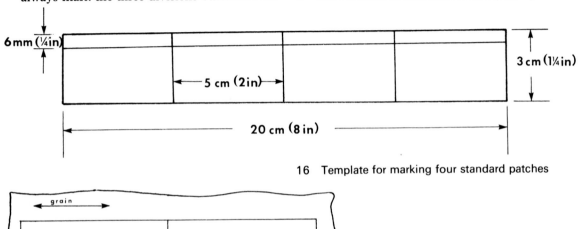

16 Template for marking four standard patches

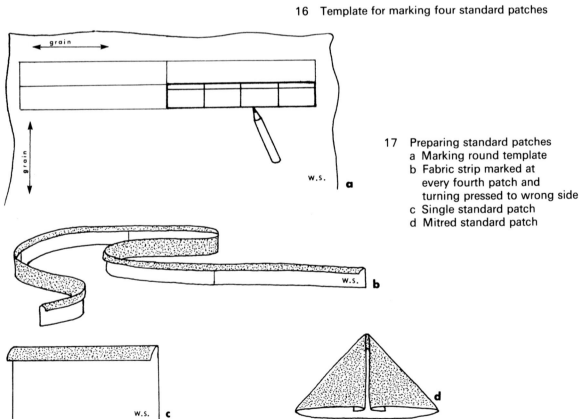

17 Preparing standard patches
  a Marking round template
  b Fabric strip marked at every fourth patch and turning pressed to wrong side
  c Single standard patch
  d Mitred standard patch

7 Divide each piece into four equal sections. This is easily done by folding in half and cutting, then folding each of the resulting two pieces in half and cutting, making four patches. The patches, excluding the turning, will now each measure 5cm (2in) by 2.5cm (1in) (*figure 17c*).

8 With the wrong side uppermost, take each patch and place the corners of the turned edge to meet at the centre of the bottom raw edge. Press. This will form a mitred right-angled triangle (*figure 17d*).

It is not always necessary to press the mitre of each patch. I have found when applying the patches that it is quicker to mark a crease line at the centre of the patch by folding it in half and rubbing the fold with thumb and index finger. The fold mark is then aligned with the marking on the backing fabric for accurate positioning. The mitre is made as the patch is stitched in place. This is especially useful when working with springy fabrics that do not stay flat after pressing or are more attractive with soft edges. Also, when preparing in quantity, the unmitred patches are very much easier to store between working sessions. I usually keep each colourway of patches in small polythene bags, the patches grouped in tens. This makes counting much easier.

18 Square patches
  a Template for four square patches
  b Folded square patch
  c Folded and mitred square patch

Square patches

For transparent, thin or easily-fraying fabrics, or for articles that require frequent washing, it is best to use a square patch.

1 Make a template in card measuring 20cm (8in) by 5cm (2in). Mark in four equal sections of 5cm (2in). Mark a central line parallel to the long edges (*figure 18a*).

2 Keeping the long edge of the template true to the grain of the fabric, draw round the template. Continue marking along the fabric to form long strips marked off in 20cm (8in) sections.

3 Mark a number of strips onto the fabric.

4 Cut the fabric into long strips on the marked lines.

5 Fold the strips in half with wrong sides together along the whole length and press.

6 Cut on the marked divisions.

7 Divide each piece into four equal sections. Each patch will now measure 5cm (2in) by 2.5cm (1in) (*figure 18b*).

8 Each patch can now be folded into a mitred right-angled triangle and pressed, if desired (*figure 18c*).

Patches for non-fraying fabrics

Leather, felt, ribbon and some fabrics that have a bonded construction do not fray and require no turnings. The patches for these fabrics are there-

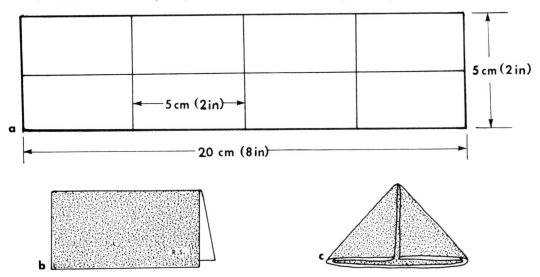

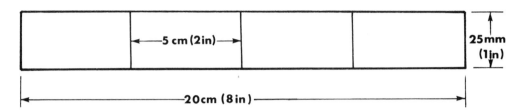

fore cut accurately to size, each measuring 5cm (2in) by 2.5cm (1in) and folded into a mitred right-angled triangle. For cutting out in quantity the cardboard template for four patches should measure 20cm (8in) by 2.5cm (1in) (*figure 19*).

Leather, felt and velvet are shown off to their best advantage if the mitre is not pre-pressed. The soft folded edges give a more attractive appearance.

19   Template for four patches requiring no turnings

You will notice that all the patches form a rectangle 5cm (2in) by 2.5cm (1in) before making the mitred fold. There are times when a smaller or larger patch is required. Whatever size of patch is required, the golden rule is that when the patch is ready for the mitred fold it should be *twice as wide as it is high*, e.g. 8cm (3in) by 4cm (1½in).

3 Method

STITCHING THE PATCHES

Alternative instructions are given in brackets for left-handed workers.

Stitching for each pressed patch

Each patch requires four stitches to hold it in place. Figure 20a shows the named parts of the mitred patch.

1 Bring the needle up through the backing fabric to where the point of the patch is to be placed.
2 Insert the needle between the mitre folds and pass through the back of the patch and the backing fabric. The stitch should be small and will lie under the folds of the mitre when completed (*figure 20b*).
3 Bring the needle up near the bottom of the right (left) edge.

4 Insert the needle through the patch and backing fabric, making a small horizontal stitch (*figure 20c*).
5 Bring the needle up through the backing fabric and the patch near the bottom of the mitre on the right (left) side.
6 Insert the needle at the left (right) side of the mitre, making a small horizontal stitch that holds the folded edges butted together (*figure 20d*).
7 Bring the needle up near the bottom of the left (right) edge.
8 Insert the needle through the patch and backing fabric making a small horizontal stitch (*figure 20e*).

On the wrong side the stitches will be quite long.

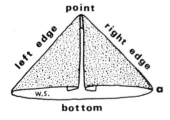
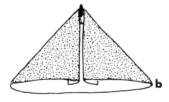

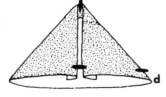
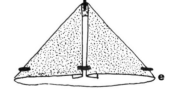

20 Stitching the mitred patch in place
a Named parts of the mitred patch
b First stitch
c Second stitch
d Third stitch
e Fourth stitch

19

The finished work will require a lining if it is to be used for an article where these stitches might catch or break.

Stitching for patches without pressed mitres

To save time and energy and to store prepared patches easily, the mitres need not be pressed (see p. 17). When making the mitred fold whilst stitch-ing the patch in place, better accuracy and control is gained by using five stitches in the following order.

1 Place the creased centre of the patch on the marked line of the backing fabric with the centre of the folded edge where the point of the patch is to be placed.

2 Bring the needle up through the backing fabric at the top centre edge of the patch.

3 Insert the needle through the creased centre line of the patch and the backing fabric making a small vertical stitch (*figure 21a*).

4 Fold one side of the mitre and bring the needle up through the backing fabric and all the layers of the patch near the bottom edge.

5 Fold the other side of the mitre and make a horizontal stitch across the two folded edges at the base of the mitre (*figure 21b*).

6 Make a stitch near the bottom of the right (left) edge (*figure 21c*).

7 Make a second stitch at the bottom of the mitre. Too long a thread would be on the wrong side if this stitch were omitted (*figure 21d*).

8 Make the final stitch near the bottom of the left (right) edge (*figure 21e*).

Positioning the patches

For the first practice piece choose four light-weight cotton fabrics in shades of one colour. You may like to use a fabric with a small print to obtain one of the shade variations. For convenience the four shades will be named, from pale to dark, A, B, C and D (*figure 22*).

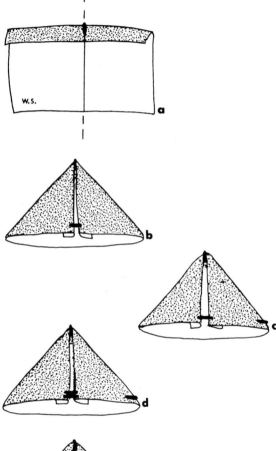

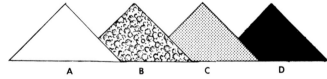

22 Four shades used for the first practice motif

21 Stitching an un-pressed mitred patch in place
  a First stitch
  b Second stitch
  c Third stitch
  d Fourth stitch
  e Fifth stitch

The star motif

1 Prepare the background fabric for a 10cm (4in) square (*figure 13*). For this first practice piece do not worry about seam allowances.

2 Cut and prepare patches. You will require – four × A, eight × B, 16 × C and 28 × D. Any extra prepared patches will be useful for further motifs.

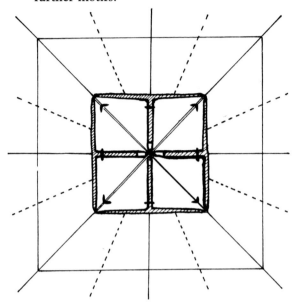

23 Star motif: four patches set in centre

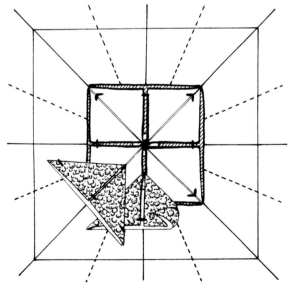

24 Star motif: commencing second row of patches, omitting right edge stitch on first patch

3 Start in the centre, using four patches of colour A. Stitching each patch in turn, position the patches so that the points all meet at the centre. The edges of each patch should be in line with the marked diagonals and the mitres with the vertical and horizontal markings (*figure 23*).

4 Take eight patches of colour B. For this first piece of work apply the patches in a clockwise (anticlockwise) direction. Omit the right (left) edge stitch on the first patch. This will be made after the eighth patch has been applied (*figure 24*). Stitch each of the eight patches in place with the points about 1.2cm ($\frac{1}{2}$in) from the centre. The distance can be judged by eye without measuring. Four patches will overlap the first row with mitres in line. The mitres of the other four will be in line with the diagonal markings. The last patch will tuck under the first and the omitted stitch can now be made. The patches will lie one over the other like a fan or hand of cards (*figure 25*).

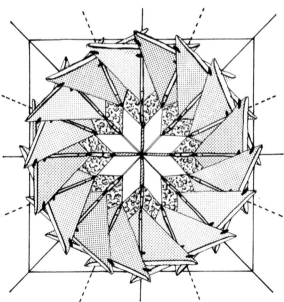

25 Star motif: second row of patches completed

5 Take 16 patches of colour C. Work in the same way as step 4, placing the patch points about 2.5cm (1in) from the centre. Eight patches must overlap the previous row with mitres in line. The mitres of the other eight will be in line with the broken markings and the points at the angles of the overlapping B patches

21

(*figure 26*). The last patch may need the bottom corner cut off if it is too long to fit flat beneath the free corner of the first patch.

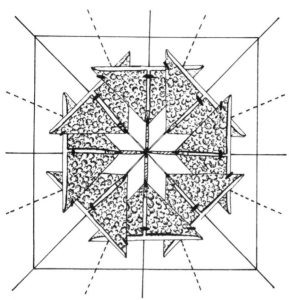

26   Star motif: third row of patches completed

6 Take 16 patches of colour D. Position them approximately 3cm (1¼in) from the centre overlapping the previous row of colour C.

27   Star motif: fourth row of patches completed, adjusting stitching at cutting line

The bottom of some of these patches will extend beyond the square. For these patches adjust the stitching position where necessary so that they are placed just inside the marked square. As before, tuck the first patch under the last, snipping off the bottom corner if necessary (*figure 27*).

7 You will now be left with four corners to complete. Using 12 D patches, arrange three in each corner (*figure 28*).

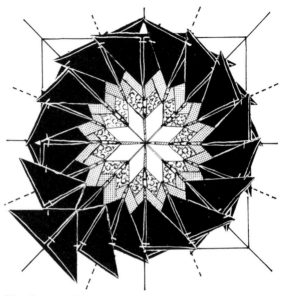

28   Star motif: one corner of the square completed

8 Cut through the patches and backing fabric along the lines of the marked square.

This star motif covers the basic method of mitred patchwork. The motif can be used for making an article (see Chapter 5 for ideas for use), or mounted as a sample for reference.

When larger squares are made, some of the corner patches can be increased in size, but always remember the golden rule: twice the width to height (see Chapter 2). To control the larger patches you can use extra stitches to hold them in place, but remember that the stitches should not show on the front of the completed work and must not extend beyond the cutting line. Larger motifs require an increase in divisions and the number of patches for each circle. The extra patches will have the mitres in line with the additional bisecting markings (*figure 15*).

29 Star motif cushion: worked with large patches in organza, silk and lamé fabrics

N.B. When making articles, remember that the outline shape marked on the backing fabric will be the cutting line and the seam allowance must have been included. All stitching must be inside the cutting line and the final visible stitches must be in the seam allowance. I have found it helpful to place extra stitches in the seam allowance to secure the edges firmly (*figure 30*). The last row of patches will cover the marked seam and cutting lines. It is helpful if each patch is trimmed to the cutting line as soon as it is stitched in place, as this allows the eye to estimate the seam allowance area more easily (*figure 31*). To aid you to check that the stitching is in the seam allowance when the patches obscure the markings, it can be helpful to have the seam and cutting lines marked on the wrong as well as the right side of the backing fabric. Marking the back can easily be done at the same time as the right side markings by using dressmakers' carbon tracing paper (*figure 32*).

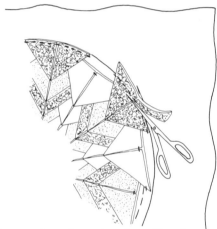

31 Extending patches trimmed to the cutting line immediately after being applied

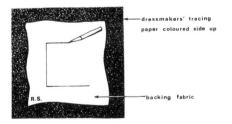

32 Marking the wrong side of the backing fabric

30 Star motif in an oval: shows additional stitches in the seam allowance

Having learnt the basic method by making the star motif, more exciting developments can now be discovered.

4 Variations

In this chapter the basic method is developed through nine different variations. Each section does not attempt to explore all the possibilities fully but offers a springboard for further discoveries.

1. CLOSE PATCHING

By making the overlaps of the patches very much closer, fascinating gradings of colour and texture can be achieved. A motif worked regularly in circles with close overlaps produces a pretty flower effect. This motif, which I call the carnation, can be seen in figure 33 and in colour plate 11. The working method is given below.

33 Carnation motif

The carnation

Use the same or similar fabrics as for the practice sample of the star motif. The patches required are: 36 × A, 36 × B, 20 × C and 24 × D. Also, prepare a 15cm (6in) circle on a backing fabric.

1 Using A set the first four patches in the centre.

2 Using B set another four patches to overlap the four A patches, mitres in line but points approximately 4mm ($\frac{3}{16}$in) from the centre.

3 Repeat step 2 using C to overlap B with points approximately 4mm ($\frac{3}{16}$in) apart (*figure 34*).

4 Repeat step 2 using D to overlap C with the points approximately 4mm ($\frac{3}{16}$in) apart. When the thread would make a very long jump on the wrong side, extra stitches can be made in the backing fabric where they will be covered by future patches.

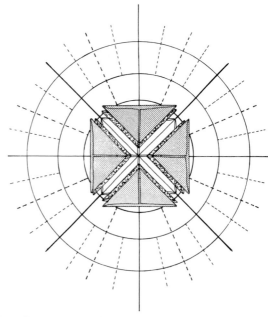

34 Carnation motif: third row of patches completed

5 Set another four patches of D with the mitres in line with the diagonal markings approximately 1.2cm ($\frac{1}{2}$in) from the centre. You will now have eight patches of D in a circle with alter-nating patches above and below one another (*figure 35*).

6 Repeat steps 4 and 5 seven times using the fabrics in the following colour order for each complete circle of eight patches: A B C A B C D.

7 Using D place another set of patches between the eight D patches already stitched. The mitres should be in line with the broken bisecting markings. Figure 36 shows this and step 8 partly completed.

8 Repeat the rhythm of the 16 D patches twice using A then B.

9 Trim and mount or use for an article. Figure 155 shows a sizable motif representing a carnation that is to be applied to a very large vestry curtain.

N.B. Unless necessary, future diagrams will omit to illustrate the stitching to give better clarity of the patch positions.

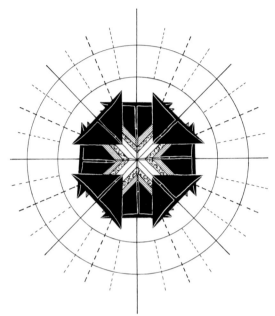

35 Carnation motif: fourth row of patches completed

2. CHANGING THE SPACING AND OVERLAPPING

Larger areas of patches can be exposed by chang-ing the spacing and overlapping. If a fabric with a special finish, colour or feature is used, it can be emphasised in this way. A pretty motif that shows this, plus a change in the regular star patterning, is a motif I call a double-barbed quatrefoil. Direc-tions for making this motif are given below and the completed motif can be seen in figure 37 and in colour plate 12.

36 Carnation motif: last three rows of patching commenced

37 Double-barbed quatrefoil motif

Double-barbed quatrefoil

Use the same or a similar set of four fabrics as for the first practice sample of the star motif. You will require the following patches: 12 × A, 20 × B, 36 × C and 16 × D. Prepare a backing with a 15cm (6in) circle.

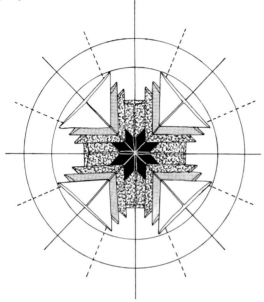

38 Double-barbed quatrefoil motif: first four rows of patching completed

1 Using D set the first four patches in the centre.

2 Using B set four patches to overlap A, mitres in line, the points approximately 1cm ($\frac{7}{16}$in) from the centre.

3 Set another four patches of B 1cm ($\frac{7}{16}$in) from the centre, mitres in line with the diagonal markings.

4 Using four patches of C, then four patches of A, set one of each colour on top of those set at step 3, with points approximately 6mm ($\frac{1}{4}$in) apart (*figure 38*).

5 Use 12 patches of D. Set four patches with mitres on the vertical and horizontal markings and points approximately 2.5cm (1in) from the centre.

6 Using 12 patches of B, repeat step 5 with points 4mm ($\frac{3}{16}$in) apart (*figure 39*). This completes the motif of a double-barbed quatrefoil that uses a 10cm (4in) circle.

To make further elaborations continue with steps 7 and 8, otherwise continue to set patches of B to the size of the shape required.

7 Using first eight C then eight A patches, points being approximately 1.2cm ($\frac{1}{2}$in) apart, set them in line with the eight broken bisecting markings.

39 Double-barbed quatrefoil motif to fit a 10cm (4in) circle

40 Double-barbed quatrefoil motif: further patching started to make a larger circular motif

26

8 Using 24 patches of C, set groups of three patches around the circle. Line up the central patches on the vertical and horizontal markings and broken bisecting markings, alternating the overlap below then above in groups (*figure 40*).

Colour plate 12 shows the double-barbed quatrefoil clearly in blue crystal organza contrasting with the fawn, brown and orange satins.

3. PATTERNS

A variety of patterns can be seen in all the illustrations of this book. Study figures 41 to 51; try producing some of them. Experiment by reversing the positions of contrasting colours. This will change the emphasis and visual appearance, producing new patterns. Continue to experiment and many more patterns will be produced. A useful way to experiment is by using cut triangles of coloured and printed paper. A little cowgum will hold them in place on a background sheet of paper but they will still be movable for a short time before the glue sets. This allows adjustments to be made to achieve the desired effect.

Fabrics with narrow printed or woven stripes offer useful pattern effects depending on their direction. Figure 41 shows a motif that I have named cross paty and shows a striped fabric used with a patterned print and a plain fabric. The stripes are placed parallel to the long edges of the patches for the cross motif in figure 42. The motif

in figure 43 has stripes used in both directions. The patterns that form crosses could be used effectively in Church embroidery. An example of this can be seen in figure 52 and colour plate 10 where a gold kid cross paty motif is strikingly used for a Bishop's mitre.

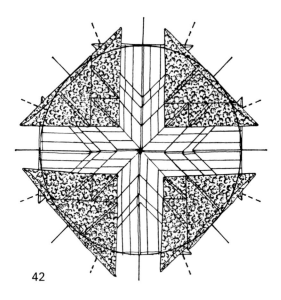

42

41   Cross paty motif

43

27

44

46

45

47

4. MANIPULATING COLOUR

Colours can be used in so many ways. They can give harmony or discord, be tones or contrasts. With the great variety of colours and patterns available in textiles the opportunities for creating many effects are endless. Colours can be bright or dull, gentle or strong, and can shade from dark to light. The patterns produced with mitred patch-work can completely change their appearance when different sets of colours are used. If a dominant colour changes position then a different part of a pattern is emphasised. The cot quilt in figure 142 (and colour plate 1) uses the same motif in every square but the two centre squares reverse the colour order. Notice how the two centre squares appear to stand out. This is due to the predominance of the light tones of colour which

28

48

50

49

51

reflect more light. Light tones and bright hues reflect the light and appear to advance towards you, whereas dark shades and dull hues absorb more light and appear to recede. By making use of advancing and receding colours, three-dimensional effects can be produced or motifs can be made to appear larger or smaller.

When planning a colour scheme do not look at one colour in isolation. Place colours together to

see the reaction of one against another. A colour can change appearance according to its position and quantity in relation to the position and quantity of other colours present. In patterned fabrics there are often small quantities of different colours which, from a distance, seem to blend together to give one general colour. If an adjacent plain fabric of one of these colours is placed next to the patterned fabric, the same colour is intensi-

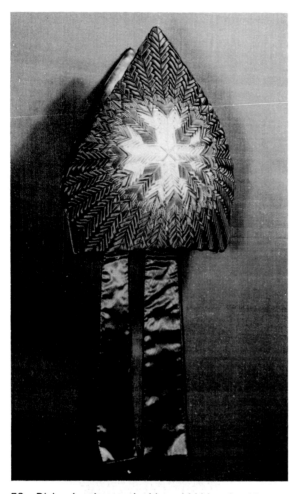

52 Bishop's mitre worked in gold kid, striped lurex jersey and satin

fied in the pattern. This can be very useful as emphasis can be given to different colours in a number of motifs when using the same patterned fabric in each. If black or white are used within a motif, the white will weaken the brightness of an adjacent colour, whereas if black is placed next to it the colour will appear lighter.

With a large-patterned fabric, the colour and textural effects seen in the fabric as a whole will be lost in the small patches. These fabrics can be used but care must be taken to select the areas of colour required. When this type of fabric is cut up for patches in the normal way, the resulting patches are very varied in their colour and textural appearance and need to be sorted into groups that have a similar appearance.

Tiny prints are very good for giving effects of colour-tone and texture. You may have already used a print successfully in earlier practice or experimental pieces. An effective motif that looks like a Catherine-wheel uses tones of four different colours and carefully positions each tone in graded order. The method for making the Catherine-wheel is given below and the sample illustrated in figure 53 appears also in colour plate 14.

The Catherine-wheel

Four different colours are used for this motif and each colour requires four tones from dark to light. Diagrams for this motif show only one of the colours in position but all the colours are used in each circle of setting patches. The four colours are labelled A, B, C and D, and the tones, from dark to light, are labelled 1, 2, 3 and 4 respectively.

Patches required for making a 15cm (6in) diameter circle:

10 each of A1, B1, C1 and D1; seven each of A2, B2, C2, D2, A4, B4, C4 and D4; and eight each of A3, B3, C3 and D3. Prepare patches, and also the backing fabric with a 15cm (6in) circle having 32 sections (*see figure 15*).

1 Set four patches in the centre: A1, B1, C1 and D1.

2 Repeat step 1, 8mm ($\frac{5}{16}$in) from the centre. All mitres in line.

3 Set four patches 8mm ($\frac{5}{16}$in) from the centre with the mitres on the diagonal markings using A4, B4, C4 and D4. The palest tone should be to the right of the darkest colour (*figure 54*).

53 Catherine-wheel motif

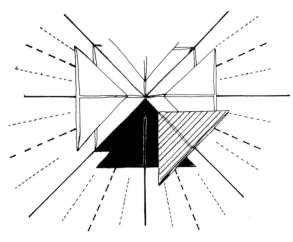

54 Catherine-wheel motif: first two patches A1, A4 set on row 2

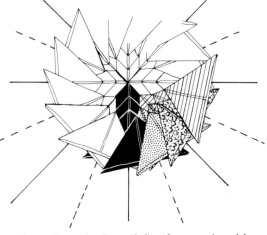

56 Catherine-wheel motif: first four patches A1, A2, A3, A4 set on row 4

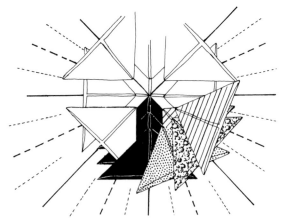

55 Catherine-wheel motif: first four patches A1, A2, A3, A4 set on row 3

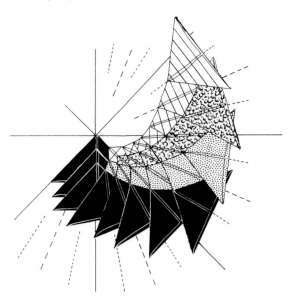

57 Catherine-wheel motif: colour group A moving one step to the right on each row

4 Working in an anti-clockwise direction, set 16 patches approximately 1.5cm ($\frac{5}{8}$in) from the centre. All dark colours numbered 1 must still be in line with the vertical and horizontal markings and tones of each colour graded to the right: A1, A2, A3, A4, B1, B2, B3, B4, C1, C2, C3, C4, D1, D2, D3 and D4 (*figure 55*).

5 Set 16 patches using the same colour rhythm but this time place the points at the angle of the previous rows' overlaps and the mitres in line with the bisecting markings. The colour rhythm will move one step to the right (*figure 56*).

6 Continue to set 16 patches in each row for five more rows, each row stepping the colour one place to the right (*figure 57*).

7 Continuing to move the colour to the right, set 32 patches for the final row.

A variation of the Catherine-wheel can be seen decorating the front of the jacket in figure 58, where tones of only one colour have been used. The left side of the jacket has the Catherine-wheel worked in a clockwise direction to balance the anticlockwise direction on the right side.

58 Jacket worked in satins and Java jersey

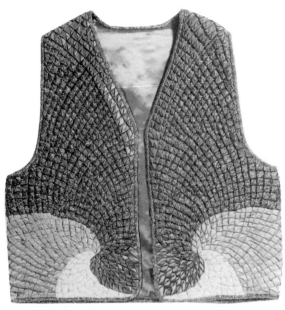

a Jacket front

59 Motif using graded tones from yellow to brown: worked in dress cottons, sheeting and Donegal tweed

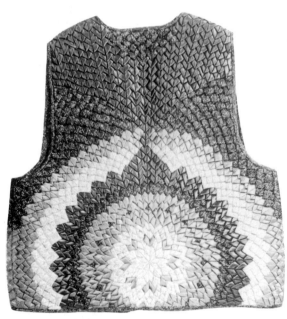

b Jacket back

5. TEXTURE CONTRASTS

There is a great variety of fabrics to give different textures, and any scrap-bag will reveal an exciting selection. Figure 59 shows Donegal tweed together with a dress-weight cotton. The thickness and the texture of the tweed contrasts well with the smooth and fine finish of the cotton. In the double-barbed quatrefoil motif used in figure 37 the smooth sheen of the satins complements the textural glitter of the crystal organza. In the Catherine-wheel (*figure 53*), plain and printed dress cottons are lifted into a more lively and exotic effect by introducing shot crystal organzas. Other illustrations show many textural fabrics.

In figure 158 velvet has been used with fine polyester lawn. The heavy velvet is difficult to handle and control but an interesting padded effect is produced. Be sure that the fabrics are suitable for the purpose of the article being made. Some velvets cannot be washed. The small turning allowance on a velvet patch could curl outwards during washing, and, because the velvet is so springy and thick, it is not really suitable for a square patch, which would normally be used to overcome this problem. In the clutch-bag (*figure 151*) velvet ribbon has been used for some of the patches, the selvedge making a very neat and well-defined mitre. Velvet ribbon is very useful as no turnings are necessary. A velvet corduroy cushion seen in figure 60 uses only one colour for all the large patches and is most successful. Changes in colour tones are achieved because the nap of the

60 Velvet corduroy cushion

61 Jewellery box: lid motif worked in gloving
leathers and silver lamé

fabric, lying in a variety of directions, reflects the light differently.

On the box lid (*figure 61*) gloving leathers and silver lamé have been used for the motif. To prevent tearing or stretching the leather when stitching, a fine glover's needle is necessary. Care must be taken to pass the needle accurately through the leather because holes made by the needle are permanent. Some varieties of lamé fray easily. If they are fine enough it is best to use a

square patch (see Chapter 2) so that all the fraying edges will be hidden either under other patches or in the seam allowance.

Try experimenting with a variety of fabrics in one motif. Choose one or two of your favourite motifs. In this way you will learn how the fabrics handle and how they appear in small or large areas within a motif. You will also be able to make more considered judgements when planning and preparing to make an article or object.

6. CHANGING THE PATCHED SHAPE

So far a square and a circle have been used as the final shapes of the motifs. In the first practice piece the corners of the square were built up after the final ring of patches reached the side edges of the square. This principle can be applied to other simple shapes, as in the large oval shown in figure 30.

The edges of the final row of patches laid in a circle themselves form a geometric shape according to the number used, e.g. a 16-sided or a 32-sided shape. If larger patches are used for the final row, or groups of patches are placed with the raw edges in line, an octagon can easily be achieved (*figures 62 and 63*).

When building up a square, if only two adjacent corners are completed the final shape will have a square and a curved end. This can be very useful

62 Final row of large patches form an octagon

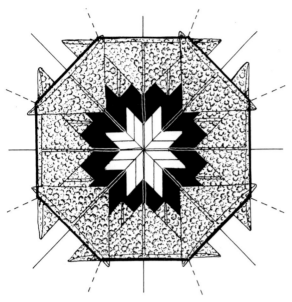

63 Final row of grouped standard patches form an octagon

for making decorative patch pockets, cosies, bags, and cases for nightwear, hankies, tights, etc.

For all the shapes always mark the seam and cutting lines on the backing fabric. Mark both sides if you find this helpful. I have found it useful, especially when marking for a garment from a paper pattern, to mark the cutting line as a

64 Final patches forming a squared and a curved edge for a patch pocket

65 Needlework box with matching needle case and pin cushion in corduroy, satins and silk

continuous line and the seam line, using a dress-maker's wheel with carbon tracing paper to produce a dotted line.

Decide where the centre of the motif is to be and then mark the vertical and horizontal lines. If the shape is part of a garment make sure that the vertical line is on the straight of grain of the fabric. Add the diagonal markings and all further bisecting lines required. Mark guiding circles from the centre point to aid the even application of the patches. Figure 66 shows the markings prepared on the yoke of a dress. You must carefully consider if any of the seam allowance is to be trimmed during the making up as this will affect the position of your final row of stitches. If you decide to bind an edge, the seam line must be changed to the cutting line and a seam line marked according to the depth of binding you will use.

A wide variety of simple shapes can be seen in the many illustrations. When planning a piece of work take care to have a simple shape to avoid too many difficulties in the making up. Especially in very small seam allowances it is best to use a number of small stitches to hold the edges of the patches firmly in place. Trim each patch to the cutting line as you progress (*see figure 31*). When the patching is completed, the backing fabric can then be cut on the cutting line ready for making up into the garment or article. When there is considerable bulk in the seam allowance, one of the best methods of finishing the raw edge is by binding (*see Chapter 6*). This method reduces the problem of bulky internal seam allowances on edges. For garments where an open seam is necessary, keep the bulk down to a minimum. If the patched piece is joined to a non-patched

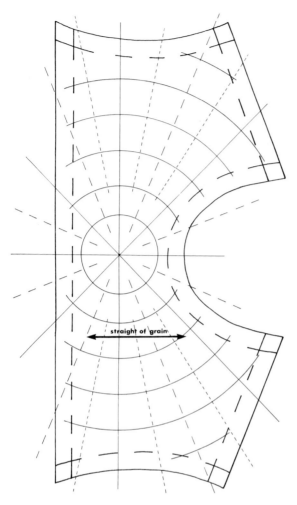

66 Dress yoke marked ready for patching

fabric, use a laid seam or a top-stitched seam so that the patched seam allowance remains flat (*see Chapter 6*). Always line the patched area of a garment. This protects the long threads and the raw edges of the last row of patches and the backing fabric. If an open seam is necessary where two patched pieces are joined together, the seam is kept flat inside the lining by being held down with Bondaweb (*see Chapter 6*).

7. THREE-DIMENSIONAL EFFECTS

Raised, padded, three-dimensional and bud-like effects can be created by varying the position of the stitches or by further folding or rolling the patches.

67 Child's dress with patched yoke

Crisp fabrics or leather can stand up on their own at the point if the folded edges of the mitre are pulled below their normal position and the point is *not* held in place. Use the leather patch or the square patch for fraying fabrics.

Method

1 Mark the centre of the patch by creasing. Do not press in the mitre.

2 Place in position and make a stitch across the crease mark. This stitch can be in any position along the crease mark depending on the raised effect required (*figure 68a*).

68 Raising the point of a leather or square patch
  a Patch held down with centre stitch near bottom

3 Fold as for a normal mitre. Stitch down in the usual way, though the central stitch should only pass through the lower fabric of the patch

and *not* through the edges of the mitre (*figure 68b*).

4 Bring the needle up at the centre near the bottom of the patch. Fold the mitre but pull the lower points below the bottom edge. Stitch in place. The distance the points are pulled will affect the height to which the top point of the patch will be raised (*figure 68c*).

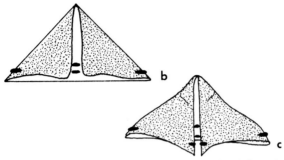

68 b Patch with mitre fold and stitched at left and right edges
   c Mitre pulled below bottom of patch and held in place

Interesting flower effects can be created. Velvet ribbon and leathers are particularly attractive. On garments it is necessary to position the raised decorations thoughtfully. For example, on the back of a jacket the points would be flattened and creased if the wearer leant against a chair back, but for a picture, hanging, or on a box they would be quite suitable. Always be sure that the fabric and effect is appropriate to the use.

Additional folding of the mitred patch adds to the patterns, lines and effects that can be created within the patching. The following method has been used together with embroidery to decorate the pencil holder in figure 149

Method

1 Place the mitred patch in position. Stitch at the point and bottom of the mitre (*figure 69a*).
2 Fold over the sides, bringing the bottom points towards the centre. They can meet or overlap depending on the effect required (*figures 69b, c and d*).
3 Stitch the bottom points in place.
4 Stitch the outer folded edges in place.

In addition to incorporating these patches within the patching on a backing, they can be used for

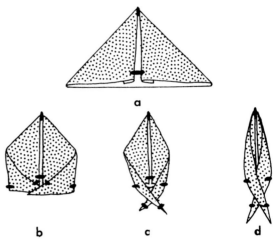

69 Additional folding of a mitred patch
   a Point and mitre held in place
   b Edges folded; bottom points slightly overlapped in line with bottom
   c Points placed below bottom of patch and overlapped
   d Points placed well below bottom of patch and overlapped

jewellery or within an embroidery. Figure 70 shows a necklet using this form where the raw edges have been neatened using the zig-zag stitch on a sewing machine.

Making more than one extra fold on each side of the mitre produces yet another effect.

70 Necklace of patches attached to silk-covered string and decorated with pearl beads

Method

1 Place the mitred patch in position. Stitch at the point and bottom of the mitre (*figure 71a*).

2 Fold the right bottom point over 6mm ($\frac{1}{4}$in). Make two further 6mm ($\frac{1}{4}$in) folds when the centre of the patch is reached. Stitch in place at the centre near the bottom (*figure 71b*).

3 Repeat step 2 with the left side.

4 Stitch the folded sides near the bottom (*figure 71c*).

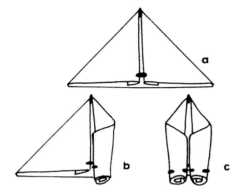

71 Multiple folding of mitred patch
  a Point and mitre held in place
  b Three folds of right side
  c Three folds of left side

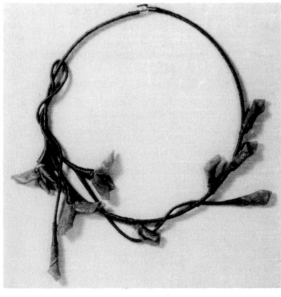

72 Jasmine necklace: buds and flowers made from mitred patches of crystal organza; silk-covered string and wire form the stalks

This patch can be incorporated into normal patching or used individually. If used individually for three-dimensional work, the raw edges can be neatened prior to folding by zig-zag machining, or oversewing by hand after folding.

In the necklace featured in figure 72 and colour plate 8 yet another method of a three-dimensional effect has been used.

Method

1 Prepare a mitred patch.

2 Starting at either the left or right point, roll the patch. The bottom edge may be kept in line or allowed to form a spiral.

3 Stitch the outer point in place and make a few stab stitches at the base to keep the roll in place (*figure 73*).

73 Rolled mitred patch

In the jasmine necklace the lower edges of the buds have been bound with silk embroidery thread that continues along the stalks. This has eliminated the need to neaten the raw edges. The stalks are lengths of string placed within the patch prior to rolling. A little glue was used to prevent the silk thread from slipping down from the wider area.

Using two patches together gives another variation. All the previous methods can be made using two patches so that contrasts of colour, pattern or texture can be seen one inside the other. This method has been used to represent the foxgloves growing up the sides of the box shown in colour plate 7 and figure 144 where leather and a printed cotton have been combined. The smooth soft leather contrasts well with the crisp cotton fabric inside that forms the delightful spotty faces of the foxgloves.

Another way to use two different fabrics for a padded effect can be seen in the cot quilt (colour plate 1) and the sample in figure 59. For this method the inner patch is folded first.

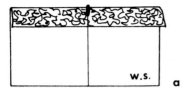

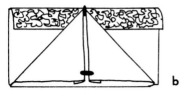

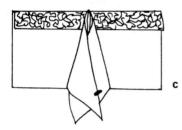

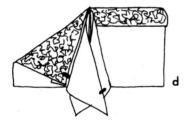

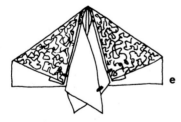

Method

1. Place the unmitred outer patch in position and stitch at the centre top (*figure 74a*).

2. Place the mitred inner patch on top of the outer patch and stitch at the top point and lower end of the mitre (*figure 74b*).

3. Make a second fold in the inner patch. Stitch in place (*figure 74c*).

4. Fold the lower outer patch so that the upper folded edge is in line with the edges of the inner patch. Stitch in place (*figures 74d and e*).

5. Bring the right then the left point of the outer patch over the inner patch and stitch in place. This forms a raised and padded bud (*figure 74f*).

This bud can be used as it is, or a further set of patches can be applied as seen within the motifs of the cot quilt.

The folding in figure 74g could be used as an individual motif within an embroidery. It could be a bird in flight, a flower, or any other imaginative form. The two final patches can be positioned to suit a variety of effects. The folded outer edges of the patches are on the bias of the fabric and can therefore be stretched to give different shapes to the final motif, especially if the fabric is soft and pliable.

By having a group of patches in various sizes, even more variations for three-dimensional effects can be achieved. For the front of the jacket shown in figure 75 the larger raised motifs used a variety of patch sizes. The number and size of the patches will vary according to the effect required.

74 Padded effect using four patches
   a Outer patch held at point position
   b Inner patch mitred
   c Second fold of inner patch
   d Outer patch left side first fold
   e Outer patch right side first fold
   f Outer patch folded over inner patch
   g A patch added to each side and overlapping folded patches

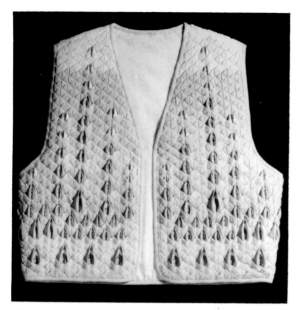

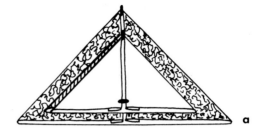

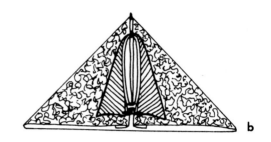

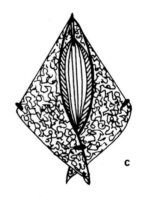

75 Peach jacket with raised patching: worked in printed Swiss cotton and slubbed voiles

Method

1 Prepare three patches, two small- and one medium-sized. I find that leaving the mitre folding unpressed gives a softer edge to the finished motif.

2 Position the medium-sized patch and stitch at the top point and near the bottom of the mitre.

3 Position the first small patch 6mm ($\frac{1}{4}$in) below the point of the medium patch. Stitch at the point and near the bottom of the mitre.

4 Position the second small patch exactly on top of the first small patch. Stitch at the point and near the bottom of the mitre (*figure 76a*).

5 Fold the second small patch edges to meet at the centre. Stitch.

6 Fold the first small patch edges to lie just beside the previous patch. Stitch (*figure 76b*).

7 Fold the medium patch edges to lie beside the previous patch. Stitch at the bottom of the centre and the sides (*figure 76c*).

If you want a much larger motif, prepare one large, two medium and two small patches, or two large, one medium and two small. By experimenting with different fabrics, sizes of patches and methods of folding, a great variety of forms can be made.

76 Raised effect with different patch sizes
  a One large and two standard patches mitred in position
  b Second folding of each standard patch
  c Second folding of larger patch

These examples give an idea of how three-dimensional work can be developed from the mitred patch. Further investigation using different fabrics, colours and textures will engender excitement in new discoveries and inspire further developments and uses.

8. WORKING IN LINES

The order of placing the patches onto a backing fabric has so far always been in concentric circles. Applying the patches in straight, curved or ran-

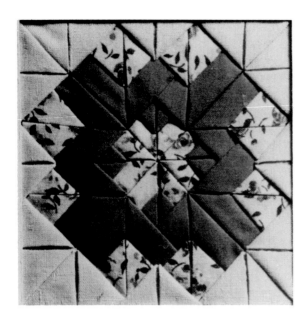

77 Sample motif: horizontal rows of patches
worked one quarter of the square at a time

dom lines offers many more varieties of patterns
and forms that can be developed. Using the
square as a basic shape, the patches can be applied
in horizontal rows working one quarter at a time.

Method

1 Draw a square on the backing fabric. For the
first attempt use a 10cm (4in) square.

2 Draw the diagonals and central vertical and
horizontal lines. Extend the lines beyond the
square (*figure 78a*).

3 Stitch the four central patches in the normal
way.

4 Using one quarter of the square only, and
working from the centre outwards, stitch the
patches in the desired pattern. Work across in
horizontal rows keeping the mitres vertical.
The first and last patches that reach the diagonal markings should have an edge exactly on
the diagonal line (*figure 78b*).

5 Carefully mark, on the unused diagonal lines,
the position of the mitre points for the remaining sections. By doing this a geometric design
will be matched accurately (*figure 78c*).

6 Work the other three quarters.

For large squares it is useful to draw some extra

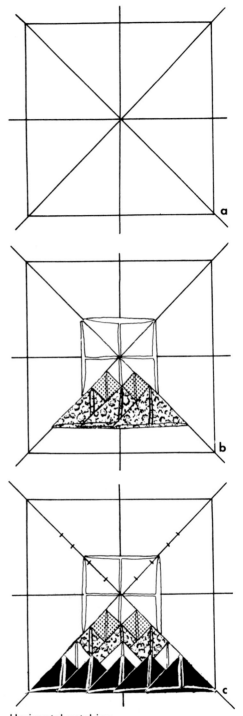

78 Horizontal patching
a Marking the backing fabric
b Four centre patches and two horizontal rows
completed
c One quarter of square completed

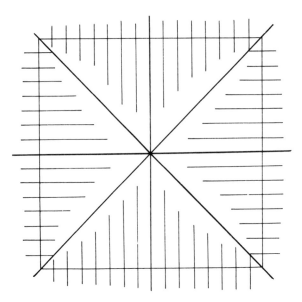

79 Markings for a large square to be worked in horizontal rows

81

vertical guide lines so that the mitres are always kept parallel (*figure 79*). Study figure 77 and figures 80 to 86 for other patterns.

Many more patterns and designs are possible, both symmetric and asymmetric, depending on the positioning of different colours, prints and textures of the fabrics used. Incorporating any of the previous seven variations will add even further to potential designs.

82

80

83

85

84

86

When using this method of applying patches, the diagonals sometimes open out slightly when the patched shape is used for padded articles such as cushions. This happens especially when using large patches, but the problem can be overcome by slip stitching the folded edges together (*see Chapter 6*), or by the addition of occasional patches being placed on the diagonals. When applying the patches on the diagonals, each quarter of the square must be completed up to the position of these patches. Once the diagonal patches have been applied, the quarter patching can continue again (*figure 87*). By using the occasional patches at the diagonals, further patterns are formed, as shown in figures 88 to 92.

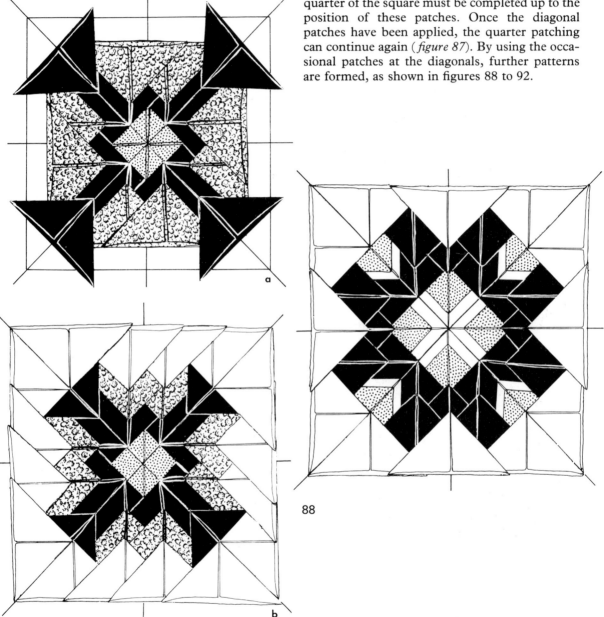

88

87 Horizontal rows with occasional patches on the diagonal
  a Working each quarter up to the position of a diagonal patch
  b Final horizontal rows of patching

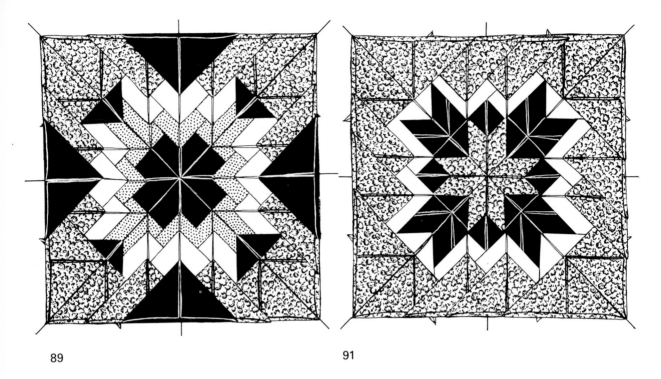

89

91

90

92 Cushion in dress-weight cottons

When applying patches in concentric circles, any simple shape can be produced covered in patches. The horizontal method of applying patches can also be used for different shapes. The clutch-bag and the jackets in figures 94, 95 and 75 are all worked by applying the patches in horizontal rows. A larger patch has been incorporated into the clutch-bag design to break the monotony and give interest to the simple pattern. Consideration must be given to the position of the first row of patches. Are the points to be in a seam allowance? Can they form part of the pattern, or can they become the edging? For the jacket in figure 95 a strip of fabric known as a facing, 5cm (2in) wide and the shape of the lower edge, was attached to the jacket first before patching commenced (*figure 93*). The patches will not penetrate into the seam allowance and the points will form part of the design without showing the backing fabric. The patching commenced at the lower edge of this jacket, whereas in the jacket in figure 75 it began at the shoulder line. The fabric strip facing was therefore applied at the shoulder area first.

94   Clutch-bag in a variety of fabrics with additional embroidery using chain stitch and couching

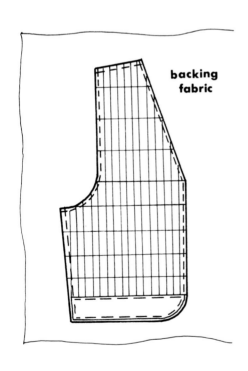

93   Facing applied to marked backing fabric

95   Pink jacket in Swiss cottons and slubbed voiles

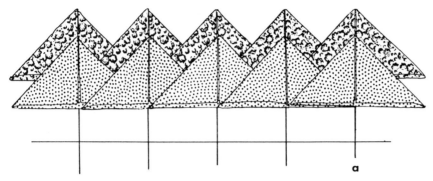

a

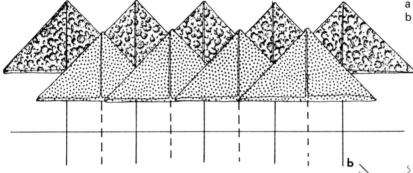

b

96 Different positions of horizontal
rows of patches
a Continuous vertical rows
b Stepped vertical rows

Method

1 Mark the backing fabric with vertical lines. If
the patches are to be positioned as *continuous
rows* (as in figure 96a), the vertical guide lines
should be no more than 2.5cm (1in) apart for
the standard size patch. If the normal size
patches are to be in *stepped vertical rows* (as in
figure 96b), mark the guide lines 1.2cm ($\frac{1}{2}$in)
apart, alternating a continuous line with a
broken line. For larger or smaller patches the
distance between the lines will vary according
to the patch sizes. A trial run on a spare piece
of backing fabric will quickly establish the
maximum distance that can be used.

2 Mark horizontal lines at regular intervals to
aid the even laying of the patches.

3 Apply a 5cm (2in) strip of fabric as a facing if
required (*see figure 93*).

4 Work the patching, trimming edges as you
progress (*figure 97*). Where half the patch
penetrates into a seam allowance, open the
patch on the seam allowance side to reduce the
bulk (*figure 98*).

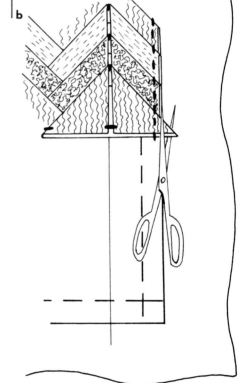

97 Extending patches trimmed to cutting line
immediately after being applied

46

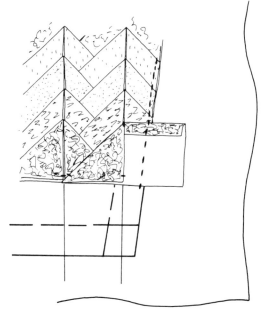

98 Reducing unnecessary bulk in a seam allowance

Figures 99 to 106 show a number of patterns. Further experiments with colour, texture, different spacing and overlapping, and three-dimensional effects will produce many more variations.

Strips of patching can be made for a variety of uses, as seen in Chapter 5. When making strips you may consider having the mitre points of the patches at the centre. The patching is then worked in horizontal rows from the centre outwards. The patches may dovetail to fit close together, as in figure 109a, or a space may be left between to allow for embroidery or any other form of decoration. A space with embroidery decoration can be seen on the christening gown in figure 108. The patching was worked directly onto the background fabric instead of a backing fabric, thus eliminating the need to apply a facing strip in the gap. The work will still require a lining to protect the long stitches on the wrong side. The strip of patching can be used as an insertion in an article and the raw edges will be in the seam allowances.

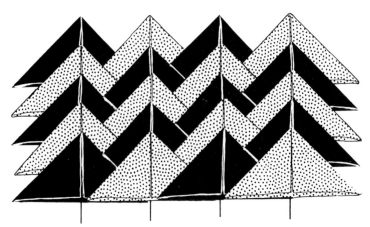

99 Continuous vertical rows worked in horizontal lines of patches from left to right

100 Continuous vertical rows worked in horizontal lines of patches alternately from left to right and right to left

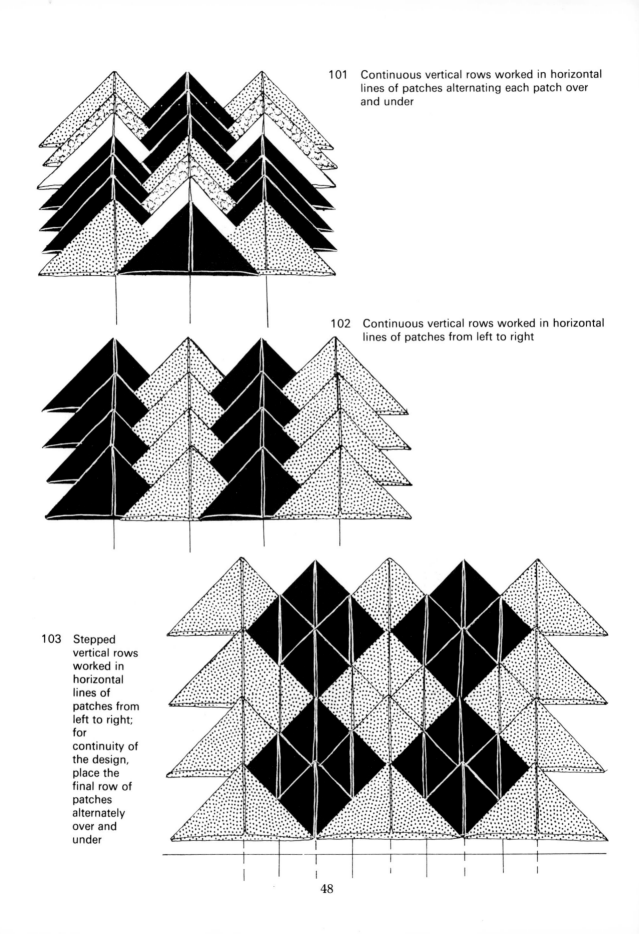

101 Continuous vertical rows worked in horizontal lines of patches alternating each patch over and under

102 Continuous vertical rows worked in horizontal lines of patches from left to right

103 Stepped vertical rows worked in horizontal lines of patches from left to right; for continuity of the design, place the final row of patches alternately over and under

1 Cot quilt

2 Pink jacket front

3 Peach jacket front

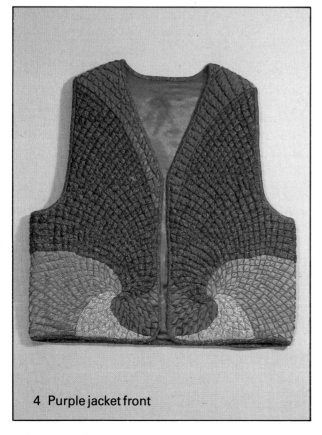

4 Purple jacket front

5 Purple jacket back

104 Stepped vertical rows: alternate horizontal lines having double patches

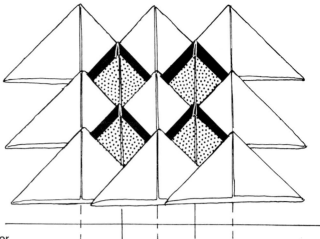

105 Both stepped and continuous vertical rows, worked in horizontal lines in one direction; for continuity of the design place the final row of patches alternately over and under

106 Continuous vertical rows having every fourth horizontal line of patches stepped

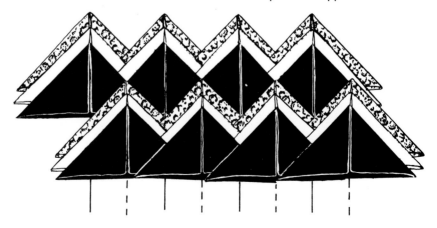

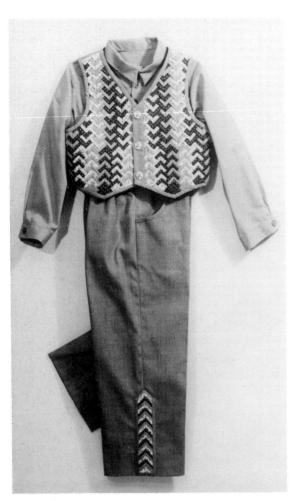

The mitre points can form a pretty pattern at the edges of the strip by working from the outside towards the centre. The raw edges of the patches will meet in the centre of the strip and they can be decoratively covered by using braids, ribbons, tapes, fabric strips or any method that is suitable and enhances the design (*figure 109b*).

If the patches can be applied horizontally they can also be applied vertically or diagonally; it is only a matter of placing the guide lines in a different direction (*figure 110*). Random guide lines are yet another way to produce designs. The landscape in figure 111 was worked using random guide lines. A few basic guide lines, taken from the main areas of the landscape, were set down first on the backing fabric (*figure 112*). The patches were then applied, commencing with the sky and working down the picture. With careful thought, free designs can be worked in many directions and commenced in different positions. For a hanging or a picture, or as in the street carnival mask (*figure 113 and colour plate 9*), the raw edges of the patches can be part of the effect. There were no problems of wear and washing to be considered as there are when making garments or quilts.

107 Boy's red, white and blue outfit: waistcoat patched in continuous vertical rows dovetailing in line with centre button; applied strip on trousers

108 Bonnet and christening gown in squared cotton voile: patching in pale green and white polyester cotton lawn and satin; embroidery worked in double back stitch and satin stitch

50

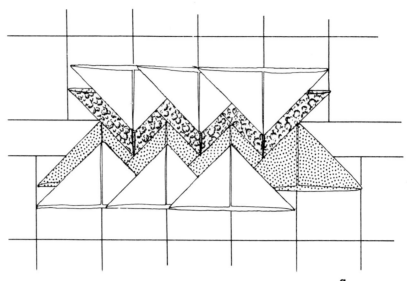

109 Alternative directions
for applying patches

a Working outwards

b Working towards a
centre and raw edges
being covered

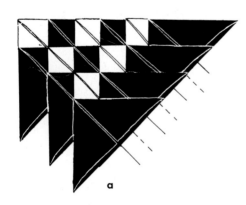

110 Alternative directions for applying patches

a Diagonally   b Horizontally

111 Landscape

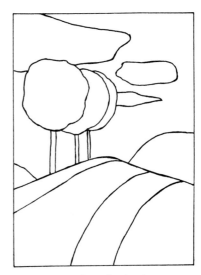

112 Guide lines for landscape

113 Carnival mask

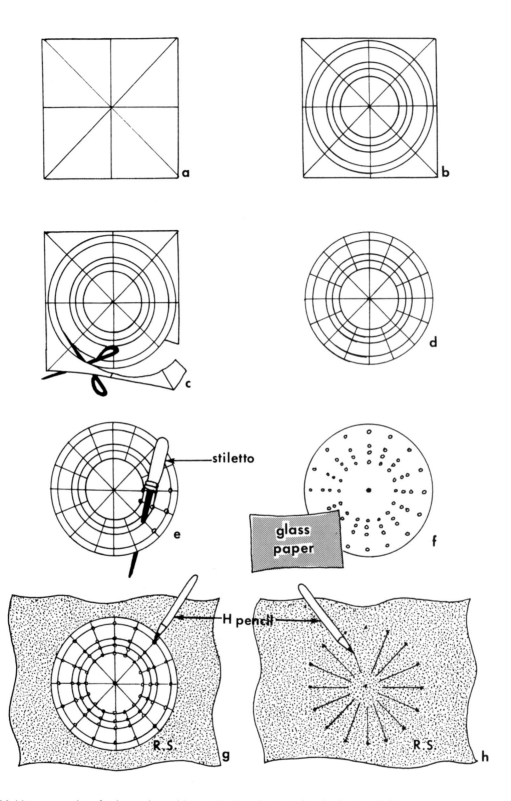

stiletto

glass
paper

H pencil

R.S.

R.S.

114   Making a template for inward patching and using it to mark a background fabric

9. WORKING CIRCLES INWARDS

This variation is like the first basic method but the patch points face away from the centre of the circle. The concentric circles of applied patches are started at the outer edge and then progress towards the centre of the circle. This gives the outer edge of the motif a neatened, pretty, petal effect. The patches will not fit snugly in the centre so a different treatment must be used to form a decorative centre. This can be done in a variety of ways including applied fabric shapes, embroidery stitches, beads, raised or padded effects. The patches are applied directly onto the ground fabric of the article or garment and therefore the backing fabric is not needed. This makes the motifs especially suited for decorating purses, bags, any fully-lined article or garment, or for combining with embroidery on panels or hangings. If used for unlined garments, careful thought and positioning are required to be sure that the stitches on the wrong side are covered by a hem or facing to prevent them from being snagged or broken.

A template is a very useful aid to marking the ground fabric accurately. An outer circle cannot be marked as it would remain visible between the points. Instructions for making and using the template are given below and reference should be made to figure 114 for diagrams of each stage.

Making the template

Materials

a   A thin but firm piece of card, 16cm (6¼in) square.

b   A pair of compasses.

c   A fine stiletto or thick darning needle.

d   A small piece of fine glasspaper.

Method

1   Mark the centre of the card. Mark the diagonals and central vertical and horizontal lines.

2   Using the centre marking and a compass, make five circles. You can make the radii any size you like but I have found the following sizes most convenient: 6.3cm (2½in), 4.5cm (1¾in), 3.8cm (1½in), 2.5cm (1in).

3   Cut the card along the outer circle.

4   Divide the circle into 16 equal segments.

5   Using the stiletto or darning needle, pierce the card at the intersecting points and the centre.

6   Turn the card over and rub away the raised edges of the holes using the glasspaper.

To mark the fabric

1   Place the template in position on the right side of the background fabric.

2   Mark the position for the points of the first row of patches and the centre by pushing a sharp H pencil or fabric marker pen through the holes.

3   Remove the template and mark the guide lines from the dots to near the centre. No markings will show after the motif is completed.

To gain experience in working inward patching it is useful to make a sample of each of the following methods. Use the same or similar fabrics as those used in your first samples of outward patching. The direction of placing the patches can be worked clockwise or anticlockwise, whichever is easiest for you and depending on the required effect.

115   Sample of inward patching method 1: centre completed using a stem stitch wheel and fly stitches

Method 1

Patches required: 16 × A, 20 × B, eight × C, four × D.

1 Mark the background fabric with 16 divisions, radius 6.3cm (2½in).

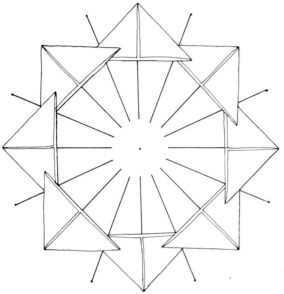

116 Inward patching method 1: first row of patches applied

2 Using A, apply eight patches at alternate markings (*figure 116*).

3 Using B, apply eight patches between those already in place (*figure 117*).

4 Using A, apply eight patches with the mitre points 1cm (⅜in) below the first set of patches.

5 Using B, apply eight patches with the mitre points 3mm (⅛in) above the intersections of the previous eight patches.

6 Using C, apply eight patches with the mitre points 3mm (⅛in) above the intersections of the previous eight patches. Omit the lower side stitch of the first two patches applied until the eighth patch is in place. Trim any lower points that may show from the previous row of patching (*figure 118*).

7 Apply a further row of eight patches, alternating B and D using a three-dimensional effect shown in figure 69d.

8 Complete the centre with a decorative finish of your choice. A variety of centre finishes can be seen in the various illustrations. For details of working see Chapter 6.

117 Inward patching method 1: second row of patches applied

118 Inward patching method 1: last row of flat patches applied

56

Method 2

Patches required: 16 × A, 16 × B, eight × C, eight × D.

1. Mark the background fabric with 16 divisions, radius 6.3cm (2½in).

2. Using A, apply 16 patches at each marking. On the first patch omit the right edge stitch if working anticlockwise or the left edge stitch if working clockwise. Tuck the last patch under the first patch and complete the stitching.

3. Using the 16 B patches, repeat step 2 but place the points of the mitres at the intersections of the previous row of patches (*figure 120*).

4. Using C, apply eight patches as step 2, but placing the mitre points at every second intersection.

5. Using D, apply four patches, mitre points 1cm (⅜in) below the points on alternative patches of the previous row (*figure 121*).

6. Using D, apply four patches in the spaces between those at step 5, making extra folds for a three-dimensional effect as shown in figure 69b.

7. Complete the centre in your own choice of finish. The worked sample of this method (*figure 119*) has a completed centre using French knots.

120 Inward patching method 2: second row of patches applied

119 Sample of inward patching method 2: centre completed with French knots

121 Inward patching method 2: last row of flat patches applied

A motif of less than 4.5cm (1¾in) radius will only require eight divisions unless narrow ribbons or very small patches are used. When using eight standard patches any position smaller than 3.5cm (1⅜in) radius requires the patches to have further

57

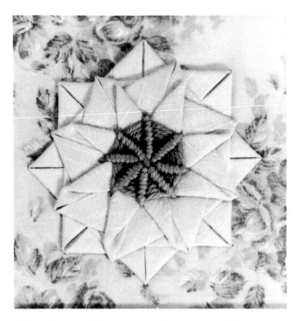

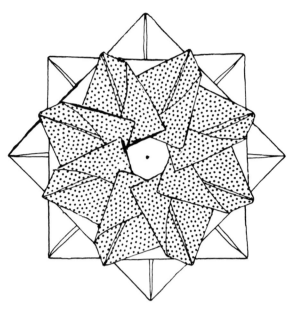

122 Sample of inward patching method 3: centre completed with a spider's web

123 Inward patching method 3: patching completed

folding. The three-dimensional effects in variation 7 are very attractive but care must be taken to cover the raw edges in the previous row of patching. Occasionally the lower points of the previous row of patches need to be trimmed to prevent them from showing, especially when nearing the centre.

Method 3

Patches required: eight × A, eight × B.

1 Mark the background fabric with eight divisions radius 3.8cm (1½in).

2 Apply eight A patches at each division tucking the last patch under the first patch.

3 On *every* patch omit the right edge stitch if working anticlockwise or the left edge stitch if working clockwise, and apply eight B patches with the mitre points at the intersections of the previous row of patches.

4 Fold over the free edge of each patch and stitch in place. This will give a windmill effect (*figure 123*).

5 Complete the centre in your own choice of finish. The worked sample of this method (*figure 122*) has a completed centre with a

spider's web. Instructions for making a spider's web can be found in Chapter 6.

Decorative flower motifs using ribbon can be worked in a similar way. The ribbon can be folded into a mitre and have the normal patch, or it can be cut longer so that long stems are formed (*figure 124*). Stitching down the edges of this shape needs a perfect matching thread. The edge stitches will be visible as they will not be covered by an adjacent patch. The edges can be left free if this is practical for the use of the article.

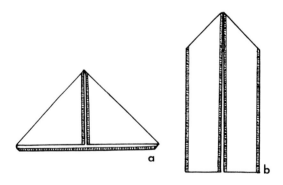

124 Ribbon used for inward patching
a Folding for a standard patch
b Folded with long stem for petal effects

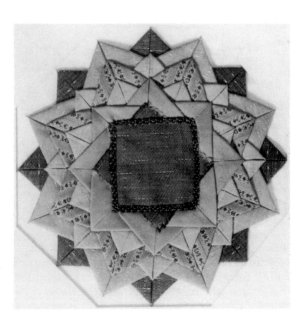

125 Sample inward patching: centre completed
with beads

126 Sample inward patching: centre completed
with appliqué and couching

Much larger motifs are workable but the back-ground fabric would be wastefully covered, and the less difficult outward method of application onto a backing fabric is more advisable. More care must be taken to consider weight and positioning of much larger motifs. As shown in the previous variations, further effects can be produced by changing the fabric colour and texture, and making additional folds to the patches. Highly decorative and inventive ways of completing the centres can add further individuality.

Mitred patchwork is still in its infancy, and therefore there is an opportunity for it to be exploited to the full. The nine variations, from controlled geometric patterns through countless varieties of fabrics, colours and textures, to random and three-dimensional application, offer potential for creative work using a small mitred patch.

7 Ideas for use

When planning to use mitred patchwork for a specific purpose, remember that the patched areas will be firm and less flexible. The fabrics used for the patches, the backing and lining must be suitable for the use and care of the final item being made. All items will be considered for their decorative effects, but wear and care will be of great importance for garments and household articles, though less important for purely decorative items.

When collecting and storing pieces of fabric for future use it is wise to attach labels to them with the fibre content and care coding. It is surprising how easy it is to forget this information. When purchasing fabric from a bolt of cloth, this information should be found attached to the fabric or printed on one end of the cardboard roller. If you are in doubt, ask the shop assistant. Friends are always generous in giving their oddments of fabrics left over from dressmaking and it is not always easy to obtain the necessary fibre and care information. If you are in doubt as to whether a fabric can be washed, test it, or save it for a non-washable item. It is better to be safe than risk having the finished article spoil the first time it is washed.

I find the best way to keep my stock of small lengths of fabrics is by grouping them into colours. I use a number of deep cardboard boxes, each containing one colour group: blacks to greys; whites to creams; browns to fawns; blues; yellows; reds; greens; oranges and purples. If the fabric is patterned or printed, I code it by the background or by whichever colour predominates. You will find that you learn a great deal about colours when sorting the fabrics, especially with the range of secondary colours – orange, green and purple. For example, it is sometimes difficult to decide whether a turquoise should be with greens or blues depending on how much blue or yellow makes up the turquoise.

For a wider range of plain colours it is useful to try your hand at dyeing. Use a white or cream fabric cut into manageable strips and dye to different tones of one colour by leaving immersed in the dye for different lengths of time. It is fun to take three different coloured dyes and, having first used them individually for colour tones, then to experiment by mixing them together in different proportions. A wonderful range of new colours can be obtained that would be difficult to find in a shop. I especially enjoy doing this with strips of pure silk. Having used the same fabric for all the dyeing, the care coding will be the same for all the colours produced. I always put a variety of yarns into every dye bath in order to have matching threads to fabric in case any other decorative textile forms are necessary to complete an item. Embroidery, macramé, quilting and many other methods can complement or contrast with mitred patchwork, but the same considerations must be given to appearance, care and wear when choosing methods and yarns.

After completing an item there may be spare patches left over. I usually keep these in small polythene bags in colour groups and store them with my small lengths of fabrics. If there are many patches of one kind, I group them in tens so that they are easy to count. Any patches made from fabrics requiring special treatment for cleaning are placed in separate bags and labelled with name, fibre content and care instructions.

127 Caftan: applied motifs with backing fabric binding edges; stem and fly stitch embroidery

128 Bridesmaid's dress and bag

GARMENTS

When selecting the styles for garments it is best to choose from simple shapes requiring little or no further shaping. Most ethnic clothes are made by joining simple geometric shapes. As the garments do not require precise fitting, they can form the basis for richly-coloured and decorative effects. The can be patched all over or in particular areas. If a commercial pattern is used for simple-shaped garments, select those patterns in sizings small, medium and large. For areas of patchwork select those parts of the garment requiring no additional shaping. If you prefer working on a frame and wish to make an all-over patching, make sure your frame will be large enough to mount sufficient backing fabric on which to work the garment part. The two sides of the front of a jacket are best worked side by side so that they match if the design is to be symmetrical. Sufficient backing fabric must be prepared on which to mark both the left and right front pattern pieces. Remember that any section which is covered with patches will need to be completely lined.

Necklines can be emphasised with a patched facing placed on the right side of the garment. Alternatively the patches can be stitched directly to the garment neckline and the stitches on the wrong side covered with a facing. The edge can then be neatened by binding, but remember that

129 Suggestions for mitred patchwork on
children's clothes

130 Child's dress and jacket

131 Child's dress with patched insertion

132 Boy's waistcoat

133 Back of Bishop's mitre

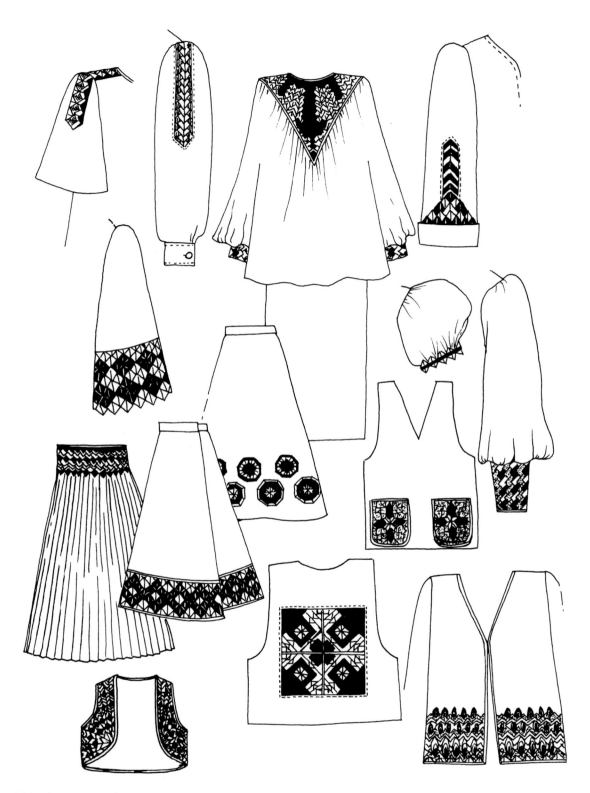

134 Suggestions for mitred patchwork on garments

no turning allowance will be necessary and the stitching line for the binding will be within the garment edge.

As seen in the dress uniform of the Guards, trouser legs look longer if the outer leg seam is emphasised. A strip of patching can be placed along the complete length of the side seam or only part way up. The little boy's outfit in figure 107 has the front of the waistcoat covered in patches and a matching strip part-way up the outside leg-seam of the trousers. The waste material from making the shirt was used for some of the patches to make a matching outfit.

When applying patched motifs or strips directly onto garments, the long stitches on the back will be protected by the garment fabric. The raw edges of the motifs or strips will require neatening. This can be done by binding before applying, or using the backing fabric and folding over to the right side. Such edges must form part of the design. The raw edges can be treated by hand or machine when being applied. A close zig-zag stitch by machine or hand-worked satin or blanket stitch will cover the raw edges. Further stitching can be added to give extra elaboration to the design.

For small areas of patching, select those parts requiring no shaping and where additional thickness is acceptable in appearance, drape and wear. For example, extra weight can be used at bottom hems, yokes and patch pockets. By making false hems or allowing larger hem allowance, patching can be done directly onto the garment and the hem will act as a lining to cover the stitches. Panels of patching can be inserted down the centre or at the crown of sleeves and down the fronts of dresses.

Sleeveless jackets, waistcoats or boleros are very successful styles of garments for covering the fronts, backs or both with patches. The backs of jackets make good backgrounds on which to build free designs or insert large motifs. When patched all over, garments become very much warmer with a firm clear shape and must be completely lined. An A-line winter skirt with little flare and no draping and with all the shaping in the side seams would be suitable for all-over patching, but not a four-gored, half or full circular or dirndl skirt. Parts of garments that benefit from additional stiffening can be patched. Waistbands, cuffs, straps and interfaced areas can be considered.

For insertions, whether in strips or shapes, the paper pattern will require adapting. Patterns must be made for the size and shape of the insertion and the unpatched parts.

To adapt a pattern

1   Select the pattern piece to contain the insertion.

2   Mark the exact position and shape of the insertion.

3   Onto fresh paper trace separately the insertion and remaining pattern pieces, using a broken line for the exact position of the insertion, and a continuous line for all the cutting lines on the pattern.

4   Add seam allowances by drawing continuous lines parallel to the broken lines. These continuous lines will be the new cutting lines. The amount of seam allowance is normally 1.5cm ($\frac{5}{8}$in).

5   Cut out the new paper pattern shapes along all the continuous lines.

Figure 135 shows a number of examples of paper patterns adapted for insertions of various shapes, in different parts of garments.

The seams in a garment need to be considered carefully. Where the garment is joined to a part that is patched, use a laid seam, laying the seam allowances away from the patched area. If two patched pieces need joining together, use an open seam, but the seam allowances will require bonding into place. This prevents the tension of the hand stitching becoming slackened and causing the patches to lift. Instructions for these seams are given in Chapter 6. When a bonded seam is used there will be additional bulk, and therefore the position of such seams must be carefully considered. Will the bulk be too great for the seam position? Loose fitting garments joined at the underarm seam are quite successful, but in a fitted skirt, allowance would have to be made for the extra thickness at the waist and hipline.

Motifs or strips can be applied directly onto ready-made garments, but, if adding patch pockets, remember that they will require lining. One way to reduce thickness when neatening the edges of motifs but still to have the effect of binding is to cut the backing fabric from a suitable fabric 1.5cm ($\frac{5}{8}$in) larger than the motif and turn over the edge as a small hem. The patches must be sewn onto the wrong side of the backing in order

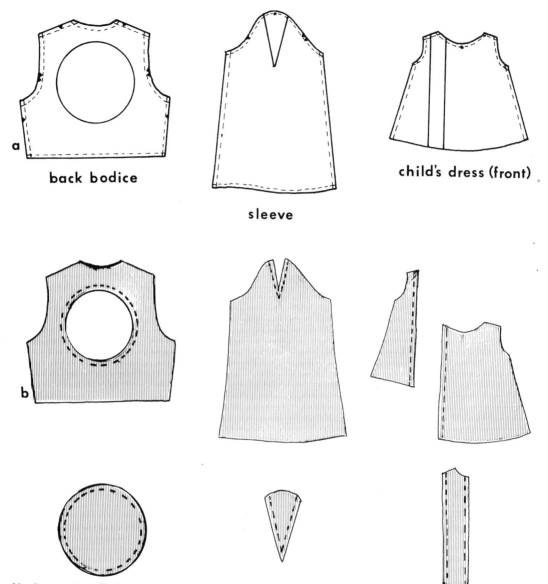

135 Altering patterns for insertions
a Original patterns b New patterns with added seam allowances

that the right side forms the hem around the notif. The motifs for the caftan in figure 127 were made in this way. The hem can be held in place by machining at the same time as the motif is stitched to the garment.

The jacket

Requirements
60cm (24in) of 114cm (45in) wide pre-shrunk, fine calico or sheeting for backing fabric.

A slate frame with tape at least 60cm (24in) long.

Patches (the jacket in figure 95 took 1810 patches).

60cm (24in) of 114cm (45in) wide fabric for lining.

3.50m ($3\frac{3}{4}$yd) binding or crossway strips 3cm ($1\frac{1}{4}$in) wide before folding.

Thread.

Pattern from figure 138 to fit size 10 to 12 (83cm ($32\frac{1}{2}$in) to 87cm ($34\frac{1}{4}$in) bust measurement).

136 Jacket front (see frontispiece for back)

137 Sketch of a jacket to be worked in stepped vertical rows

138 Pattern for jacket

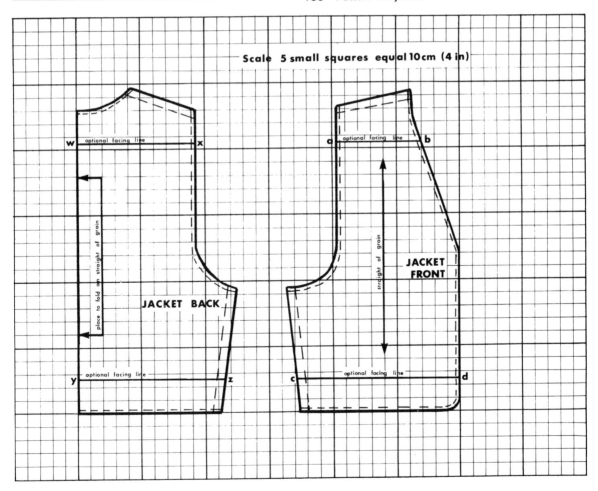

Scale 5 small squares equal 10cm (4 in)

w — optional facing line — x

place to fold on straight of grain

JACKET BACK

y — optional facing line — z

a — optional facing line — b

straight of grain

JACKET FRONT

c — optional facing line — d

Preparation

1 Cut a piece of backing fabric for the two fronts 51cm (21in) long by 61cm (25in) wide. Mark onto the fabric the left and right front pattern pieces, having 1cm ($\frac{3}{8}$in) space at the centre between the front edge cutting lines. Mark all seam lines. Shoulder and side seam allowances are 1.5cm ($\frac{5}{8}$in), armhole and outer edge seam allowances are 4mm ($\frac{3}{16}$in).

2 Cut a piece of backing fabric for the back 51cm (21in) long by 50cm (20in) wide. Make a crease line down the centre along the length. Place the centre back of the pattern on this crease line and mark the pattern and all the seam lines.

3 Mark guide lines for patching.

4 Prepare the patches.

5 Frame the backing fabric marked for the fronts. If necessary, for your chosen pattern, attach fabric facing strips to lower or shoulder edges positioning as shown on the pattern in figure 138 at w–x, a–b, or y–z, c–d.

6 Begin the patching. Do not allow one side front to progress faster than the other. This helps to keep the spacing and matching at the front opening accurate. Work clockwise on one side and anticlockwise on the other if the patching is in concentric circles, or from the centre front towards the sides if patching is in horizontal rows.

7 Remove the fronts from the frame when complete. Remember to trim the patches to the cutting line as you progress and not at the end.

8 Frame the backing fabric marked for the back. Apply any facings necessary. Work the patching. Take care to consider any matching of colours and patterns at the side and shoulder seams. Work from the centre back towards the sides if patching is horizontal.

9 Remove back from the frame.

10 Cut the backing fabric along the cutting lines.

11 Press the fronts and back on the wrong side if necessary, taking care not to catch any stitches.

12 Place the jacket parts onto the lining fabric on the correct grain, with wrong sides together. Cut out the lining.

Making up

1 Using an open seam join the side and shoulder seams of the jacket.

2 Join the side and shoulder seams of the lining using an open seam.

3 Press all seams open and flat.

4 Hold down the seam allowances of the jacket only by using 1cm ($\frac{3}{8}$in) width strips of Bondaweb.

5 With wrong sides together, pin the lining inside the jacket, matching seams and edges. A little trimming may be necessary.

6 Carefully tack all layers together along the seam lines, round the armholes and the outer edges. Remove all pins.

7 Apply binding to armholes and outer edges.

Directions for seams, bonding, and binding are given in detail in Chapter 6.

HOUSEHOLD ARTICLES

Within the home there are so many ways in which mitred patchwork can be used for a number of articles that will enhance the surroundings decoratively, give comfort, and also be practical. Use can be made of the characteristics of this method of patchwork which, because of the folding, traps pockets of air, thus retaining warmth. Any article that requires the retention of warmth would be ideal. Tea- and coffee-pot cosies, bed covers and sleeping bags are typical examples. With the addition of wadding, further warmth can be incorporated into an article. Patches can be used all over, applied or inserted in strips or motifs. When planning, it is important to consider how the raw edges are to be treated, bearing in mind that it is easier to retain the patched areas flat without turning them back. When marking the jacket described previously, the few seams used had to be bonded to prevent the tension of the hand stitching from becoming loose. It is therefore less bulky and simpler to apply another fabric to the raw edges. This can be done by binding, inserting or appliqué. These processes are described in Chapter 6.

Bed linen can be very effectively decorated along edges with strips, with single rows of patches, or small motifs. The hems can be used as a lining to cover the hand stitching. Many bed-heads are upholstered and are both difficult to

clean and need changing when new colour schemes are required. Loose covers, that can easily be pulled on and off for laundering along with the normal washload, offer an opportunity to be adventurous with mitred patchwork. The area is large enough for you to be impulsive in designing and yet not as awesome as a full-size bedspread or quilt. A cot quilt is a manageable size on which to try some ideas, and instructions are given for making the cot quilt in figure 142 later in this chapter. The applied patches produce a firm fabric which is very useful for making dust covers for electrical appliances in the kitchen, to tone or contrast with the kitchen colour scheme or echo patterns in dishes, utensils, pottery or tiles.

In the bathroom, where water needs to be absorbed, patches made from pure cotton are ideal for use on bath and basin mats and toilet seat covers. Roller blinds can have strips at the bottom edges or motifs decoratively arranged. They can be applied or attached with Velcro strips for easy cleaning, especially if they are used on a kitchen blind where, no matter how careful you are, splashes of grease and a variety of stains and dirt seem to appear from nowhere. Remember to place the fluffy part of the Velcro on the applied patch-

139 Christmas table-runner: the two movable mats have adapted cross paty motifs to form pairs of crossed crackers

140 Landscape cushion: centre worked in appliqué and machine embroidery

69

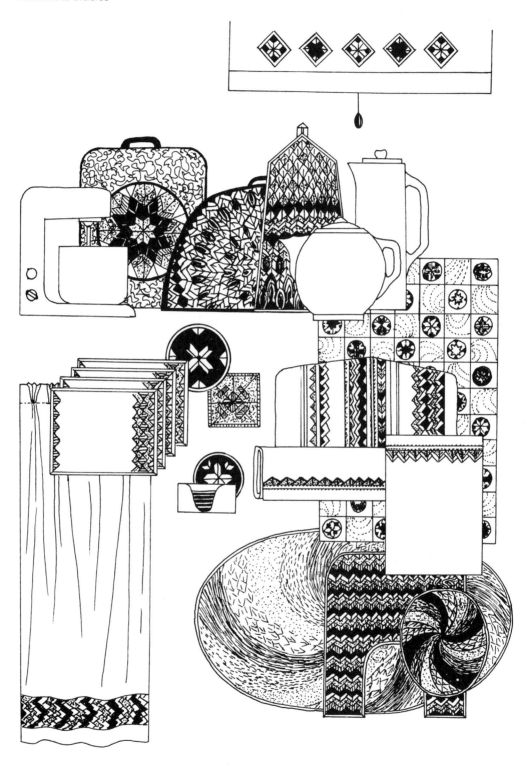

work, otherwise the hooked part would catch on other articles during washing.

Mats are required for a variety of household uses – table linen, dressing-table sets for the bedroom, protection under plantpots, and for hot and cold drinks. Do not use three-dimensional effects where pots and plates must necessarily sit firmly in place. Sets of coasters are most attractive and quick to produce. Contained in a holder, they make unusual and useful Christmas gifts.

Cushions are an ideal subject for mitred patchwork. They are a good size, being large enough to give scope for experimenting with different sizes of patches, trial of different types of fabrics, and exciting designs. They are small enough not to be daunting and are easily made up for completion.

The cot quilt

Approximate finished size 75cm (30in) by 100cm (40in).

Requirements
12 mitred patchwork motifs 20cm (8in) square. 1cm ($\frac{3}{8}$in) seam allowance is included on all edges.

142 Cot quilt

1.50m ($1\frac{5}{8}$yd) of 115cm (45in) wide fabric for the back of the quilt and the front strips. The spare fabric will give about 90 standard patches. If more patches are required for including in the motifs, extra fabric should be purchased.

79cm (31in) by 102cm (40in) polyester wadding, 2oz weight.

Preparation
1 Using tailors' chalk, mark on the fabric the back, three long strips, and eight short strips. Measurements and layout are according to the chart in figure 143.

2 Cut out the pieces on the marked lines.

Making up
1 Prepare the back by pressing 1cm ($\frac{3}{8}$in) to the wrong side of the fabric on all edges.

2 Press a second fold to make the front surrounding hem by turning 7.5cm (3in) of the back to the wrong side of the fabric on all edges.

3 Make a mitred seam at each corner (*see Chapter 6 and figure 168*).

4 Put the back onto a flat surface with hem uppermost.

5 Place the wadding on top of the back, tucking it under the side hems. Take care that the wadding is not wrinkled and fits correctly up to the fold edges and into the corners.

6 Pin the wadding in place at the centres and corners of the hems. Check measurements.

7 Prepare the eight short strips by pressing 1cm ($\frac{3}{8}$in) to the wrong side of the fabric on the long edges only.

8 Prepare the three long strips by pressing 1cm ($\frac{3}{8}$in) to the wrong side of the fabric on the long edges only.

9 Position the patched motifs, tucking them under the side hems by 1cm ($\frac{3}{8}$in) and having 3cm ($1\frac{1}{4}$in) gaps between each motif, to give four rows of three motifs. Pin carefully in position, and check measurements.

10 Position the eight short strips between the motifs lengthwise, covering the motif edges by 1cm ($\frac{3}{8}$in). Pin carefully in position and check measurements. Tack in place.

11 Position the three long strips between the motifs across the width, covering the motifs

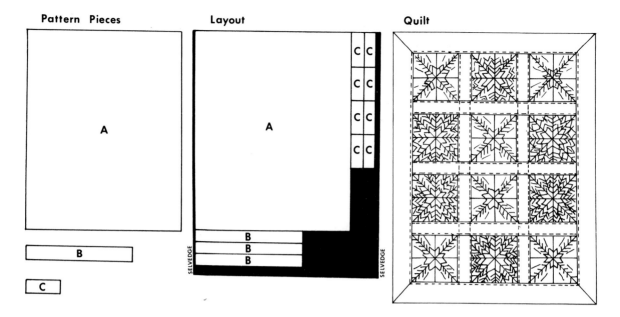

Pattern Pieces   **Layout**   **Quilt**

A

B

C

A

A

C C

C C

C C

C C

B
B
B

SELVEDGE

SELVEDGE

143   Pattern and layout for cot quilt. Three pattern pieces: A, B, C: A Back – cut one, size 96cm×119cm (38in×47in) B Long strip – cut three, size 66cm×7cm (26in×3in) C Short strip – cut eight, size 20cm×7cm (8in×3in)

and raw edges of the short strips by 1cm ($\frac{3}{8}$in). Pin carefully in position and check measurements. Tack in place. Remove all pins.

12   Tack again along edges of strips starting from the centre of the quilt and working to the outside hem. Make sure the needle passes through all layers of fabric from the front to the back at every stitch.

13   Tack along the hem edge through all layers of fabric.

14   Remove any pins.

15   Machine near all the folded edges of the strips, commencing at one side hem and continuing to the opposite hem edge. Fasten off machining by either knotting ends on the back or whipping back (*see Chapter 6*).

16   Machine the hem edge. Overlap the machining at the start and finish by 2.5cm (1in). Cut thread ends close to the fabric.

17   Remove all tacking.

CONTAINERS

If you enjoy making boxes, then mitred patchwork is a most effective method of decoration. Patched motifs set into lids, or applied patches using any of the variations in Chapter 4, can be used around the sides. The box in figure 144 has folded patches to represent foxgloves growing up the sides of the box. The octagonal box in figure 147 has two patched motifs, one decorating the outside of the lid and another inside. Both these boxes are shown in colour plate 7. The patching should be worked on the ground fabric before being applied to the box. It is therefore important to consider the proportion of patched areas to the background fabric before making the box. Border patterns of patches need to be carefully planned so that they are continuous around the sides of the box, matching accurately at any seams or box joins. Some stitches for the patches may have to be completed after a seam or join has been made so that the continuity of the pattern is not broken (*figure 145*). For box lids it is easier to set a motif beneath a fabric-covered window. This eliminates the problem of turning bulky edges round the box cardboard. Figure 146 shows how a motif can be mounted inside a fabric-covered window for the top of a square box lid.

It is very easy to overdo the patching and the general appearance of the completed box becomes too fussy. Therefore it is advisable to plan the work carefully before cutting any fabric or box

6 Group of bags

7 Group of boxes

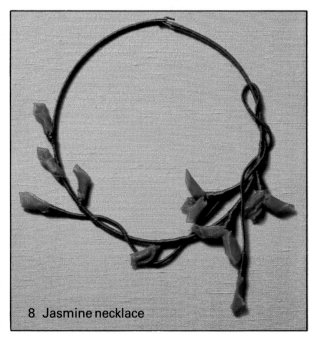

8 Jasmine necklace

9 Carnival mask

10 Bishop's mitre

11 Sample carnation motif

12 Sample double-barbed quatrefoil motif

13 Sample cross paty motif

14 Sample Catherine-wheel motif

144 Foxglove box worked in gloving leather and printed dress cotton on silk background

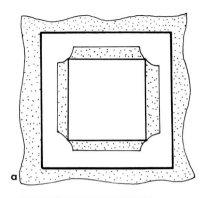

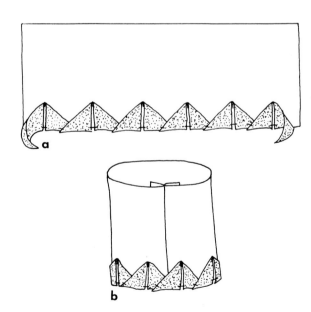

145 Continuity of patching over a seam
    a Unstitched patches near seam prior to seam being made
    b Patches stitched after seam completed

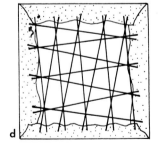

146 Mounting a motif for a box lid inside a fabric covered window
    a Wrong side of covered window card. Inner edge of fabric glued in place
    b Patched motif in position on box lid
    c Covered window card placed over box lid
    d Fabric pulled to wrong side and laced

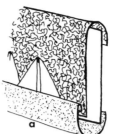
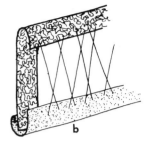

148 Binding the raw edges of patches from the outside of box
  a Binding stitched to patching then turned round cardboard
  b Binding laced to outer fabric

147 Box: inside lid decoration worked in organza, satin and cotton fabrics

foundation card. A mock-up of the box made from stiff paper or thin card is a good way to test ideas. Triangles of coloured paper can be cut from magazines, giftwraps or gummed paper to represent the patches. Experiment with proportion, quantity, position, repeating patterns, motifs, and different sizes of patches. Other forms of decoration you may wish to use can also be planned on the mock-up.

When patching is bulky at the edges and too difficult to turn behind the card of the box, the raw edges of the last row of patches should be placed exactly at the edge of the box. The raw edges can then be covered in different ways. The lining fabric can be pulled to the front and folded over the raw edges. The pencil holder in figure 149 has a knitted velvet lining pulled to the front. The characteristic stretch of this fabric has been used to make the decorative edging. An alternative finish is to bind the raw edges, but instead of turning the binding to the wrong side of the fabric it is turned over the edge of the cardboard and used when lacing the fabric into place (*figure 148*). The effect of both these methods on the final appearance of the box can be considered at the mock-up stage since a border line along an edge can make a difference to the balance of the design. Sometimes attractive results can occur quite by accident during the making up of a box. As long as consideration is given to the balance and proportion of the box's appearance, this can be an unexpected bonus.

The method of opening the box is important as the patches must not interfere with the free movement of the lid. If the lid is gripped around the edges or raised by means of a tassel, knob or tag, care must be taken not to have patches where they will interfere with the smooth opening and closing of the box, or where they will become worn too quickly. Leather patches are effective on boxes. Off-cuts of soft kid or gloving leather can sometimes be obtained and are especially suitable, but remember to use the template for non-fraying fabrics.

Very delicate, exotic or highly-textured fabrics can be used, also non-washable fabrics. There is not the concern for suitability of wash-and-wear that there is when making garments or household articles. The pencil holder in figure 149 illustrates the use of fabrics that would shrink and distort in washing but are very hard-wearing. It also shows the addition of surface stitchery, for here are opportunities to combine other forms of decoration with the patching. Carefully plan all the decoration at the mock-up stage so that the design is well-balanced and not over-ornate. Silver or gold kid patching combined with metal-thread embroidery would make a very rich decoration for a jewellery box, the smooth leather contrasting well with textured metal-thread work.

Under-padding to raise a motif into a dome is particularly effective for box lids. A padding is prepared to sit beneath the motif using layers of felt, or else kapok can be stuffed between the patched motif and the lining, taking great care not to pull the stitching. If the motif is raised, the centre patches sometimes draw apart and allow the backing fabric to show. If this does not detract from the design and colouring of the motif it will not matter, but if it does matter, a piece of fabric

149 Pencil holder: calico patching with satin and knot stitch worked on hessian; velvet jersey lining

Light but serviceable fabrics should be used to form an attractive but not heavy decoration. Fabrics left over from making garments for special or everyday wear offer an opportunity to make bags to match and produce an attractive ensemble. Colour plate 6 shows some examples of bags.

Fastenings must be positioned so that they are not placed on patches, or else the stitching that holds a patch in place may become strained and break, causing many patches to be loosened. As bags, purses and sachets are lined, there are no raw edges exposed inside. This makes them ideal subjects for mitred patchwork. The lining will cover and protect the long stitches on the wrong side of the patched areas.

The patching makes a firm fabric, which is another advantage, as many containers are reinforced with a stiff interlining. By using a mock-up, the design of shape, size, patching, fastening and size of opening can be planned, as for boxes. Use a lighter-weight paper rather than stiff paper or thin card. This is more suitable because it is more flexible when testing pleating, darts, folding and gathering, which should be kept to a minimum in the areas of patching. Gussets can be planned and positioned. The mock-up solution can be used as the basis for making a paper pattern.

One of the most successful ways of assembling, joining and neatening raw edges of bags, purses and sachets is by binding the edges together. The lining can also be contained within the binding. This is a great advantage as it results in a perfectly-fitting lining. The order in which the bindings are attached to different parts of an article must be planned carefully so that no raw edges are left exposed. It is frustrating to have to unpick in order to neaten a forgotten edge.

should first be sewn down at the centre of the backing fabric before any mitred patches are laid down. The separation can be encouraged to give a special effect in the centre. When working the centre of the Bishop's mitre (*figure 52*) a square of dark blue satin was applied in the centre of the backing fabric before the gold kid patches were sewn down. As the leather had soft folds, small spaces between the patches revealed the blue beneath, giving greater emphasis to the centre of the cross.

Planning bags, purses and sachets needs careful thought with regard to the final use. The size of the opening for inserting whatever is to be contained is important. It must relate to the size of hands or fingers and the articles to be placed inside. The weight of the bag is another important aspect to be considered. A shopping bag is heavy enough when filled with purchases, and therefore the patching must not add too much extra weight.

The clutch-bag

Requirements

Patches: 180 patches were used for the design on the front and back of the bag in figure 151.

Backing fabric for patching: 40cm (16in) by 25cm (10in) marked with cutting line, notches, seam lines, hinge position, guide lines for patching.

Outside fabric: one front, one gusset, one hinge, 1.50m (1¾yd) crossway strip 3cm (1¼in) wide.

Lining fabric: one back and flap, one gusset, one front.

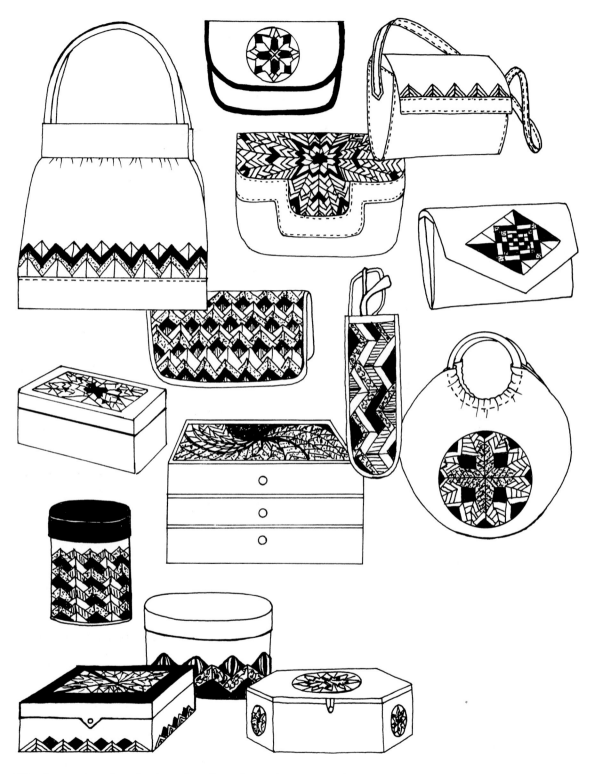

150 Suggestions for mitred patchwork as decoration on containers

Firm sew-in interfacing: one hinge.

Medium sew-in or iron-on interfacing: one back and flap, one front.

1 press stud.

Thread to match the outside fabric.

Thread for the patching.

Pattern from figure 153.

151 Clutch-bag worked in velvet ribbon, satin, velvet jersey and cotton fabrics

152 Sketch of clutch-bag

Preparation
1 Work two patchwork motifs, one for the back and one for the flap. Allow the raw edges of the patchwork to meet at the centre of the marked hinge position.

2 Work herringbone stitch across the raw edges on the hinge (*see figure 175*).

3 Cut out the back and flap on the cutting line.

4 Using tailor tacks (*see figure 181*), mark the position of the press stud on the outer fabric front and the lining fabric flap, and also all the balance marks on the front, back and flap, and the linings.

Making up
1 Trim away the seam allowance on the long edges of the hinge interfacing. Remember this is only 5mm ($\frac{1}{4}$in).

2 Tack the hinge interfacing to the wrong side of the hinge outside fabric.

3 Turn the seam allowance on long edges of the hinge to wrong side and tack.

4 Tack the hinge in place on the back and flap covering the herringbone stitch. Match the notches and the folded edges to lines a–b and c–d. Using a large, straight, machine-stitch, stitch near to the folded edges. Remove tackings.

5 Tack or iron-on the medium-weight interfacing to the wrong sides of the back and flap, and the front.

6 Tack the lining to the back and flap, the front and the gusset, having wrong sides together and matching balance marks.

7 Bind the top edge of the front.

8 Bind the two short edges of the gusset. (Instructions for binding can be found in Chapter 6.)

9 With linings together, tack the front to one long edge of the gusset matching the balance marks. Machine on stitching line. Snip the gusset at curves in the seam allowance.

10 Bind together the front and gusset.

11 With linings together, tack the back to the free long edge of the gusset, matching balance marks. Machine on the stitching line, continuing the machining around the flap. Snip the gusset in the seam allowance at the curves.

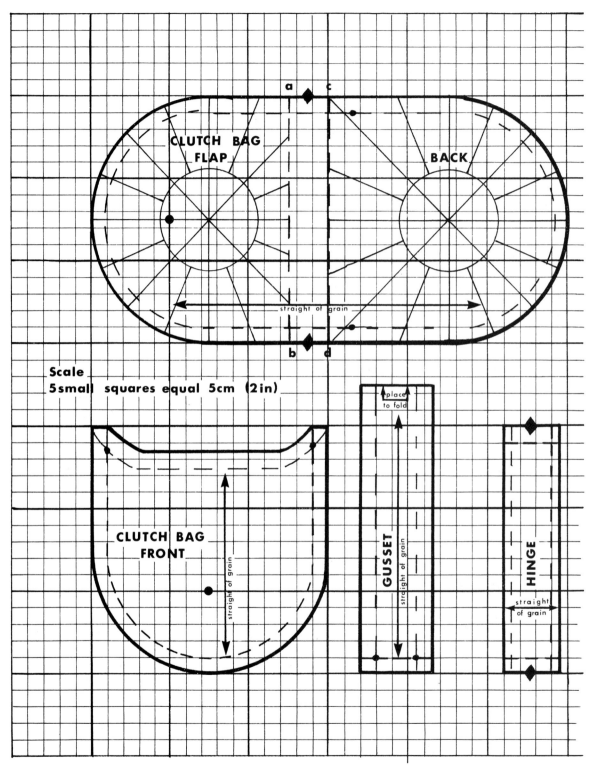

153 Pattern for clutch-bag

154   Suggestions for decorations using mitred patchwork

12 Beginning at the centre back, bind the raw edges all round the back and flap.

13 Attach the press stud at the marked positions. Do not allow the stitches on the flap to penetrate through the patches.

14 Remove all tackings.

DECORATION

Patching purely for decorative effects gives the opportunity to use many varieties of fabrics, sizes of patches and freedom to experiment. It may not be necessary to be restricted by having to consider washing and wearing; what really matters is obtaining the effect required. The carnival mask in figure 113 uses the patches freely. There has been no concern about fraying edges as they form part of the effect required. Woven fabrics cut without turnings, as for a leather patch, can have the mitre edges frayed to give a very different effect to the patch. Mixing very different fabrics together, from organza to heavy velvets, from nets to P.V.C., can be used to achieve a required effect. The patchwork can also be incorporated in a mainly embroidered piece of work.

When planning a wall-hanging or a panel it is important that the general effect does not become too busy. Too many variations in one piece of work can cause confusion to the whole appearance. There should be a balance of colour, pattern

155 Large carnation motif to symbolise love, one of a number of motifs to be applied to a large vestry curtain

and texture to give a sustained interest to the viewer without either confusion or boredom. Large pieces of work must be planned carefully for the overall effect, as this can become forgotten when actually working the details. Stand back from the work as it progresses so that it is seen from the correct distance. The effects produced from small details can encourage closer inspection, but the first impression must hold the viewer's attention sufficiently for this to happen. The framing of a panel is important and should be given careful consideration. Wood edgings can be covered with fabric to match a fabric in the panel. There are many mouldings available in a variety of finishes. Choose one that will enhance but not detract from the work. I prefer to mount my work myself, but cutting accurate mitres for the corners can be tricky. Fortunately some suppliers will provide the mouldings to any size with the mitres already cut.

With more freedom in the direction of the patching and less concern for wear and care, many sources of inspiration for a design can be used. Linear shades and tones of colour can be seen in seasonal landscapes or dramatic sunsets. Some animals and birds afford obvious interpretations of texture and pattern. The hedgehog or the armadillo would be fun subjects for a hanging in a child's bedroom; birds' feathers are arranged in overlapping sequences and have beautiful patterns: both can be translated for mitred patchwork. Collect pictures from magazines, or, better still, take photographs yourself of the things that interest you to build a source of inspiration. As your interest grows the more sources you will find that can be used as an inspiration for design.

Jewellery is always fun to try: necklaces, bracelets, pendants, brooches, etc. Little equipment is required and work can progress in your lap or on a small table. A good fabric glue is essential. Choose one that is transparent and dries quickly. Test on a variety of fabrics to find the one most suitable and easiest for you to handle. If a swing-needle sewing machine is available, edges of patches can be neatened, if necessary, with a continuous zig-zag stitch (*figure 157*), the patches then separated as required. Three-dimensional effects are particularly useful for jewellery. The base of the patches can be glued and/or bound with thread to give bud and flower effects. Clasps, brooch pins, studs, connecting rings and metal loops are useful articles for giving a professional finish to jewellery and are known as *findings*. They can usually be

obtained from a supplier of beads and sequins or a
merchant dealing in rod and sheet metals for
jewellery crafts people. Miniature purses worked
with very small patches and hung on a cord,
chain, or metal loop make very attractive neck
decorations. A metal loop and string were bound
with silk thread to complete the necklace in figure
72. Necklaces can be formed like collars. If a
binding is used to finish edges, it can continue
beyond the patching to become a rouleau which
can then be tied in a bow or fastened with a hook
and eye, and become a bracelet, necklace or hair
decoration.

Groups of single motifs can be used for decoration. Two motifs can be joined together back-to-
back or each motif lined. They can be used for
decorating a Christmas tree, or become a ceiling
mobile. If the inside is filled with sweet smelling
herbs, lavender or pot-pourri, it can be hung on a
hanger as a pomander. A piece of fabric should be
placed at the centre of the motif's backing fabric,
because the filling will cause a dome and may part
the centre mitred patches. Take great care if
filling directly between the motif and the back
that the stitching is not pulled.

156 'Adventure Playground': patchwork in primary
colours; figures, silk-covered string

157 Continuous zig-zag stitch to neaten raw edges
of many patches

The lavender bag

Requirements

One circular patched motif 15cm (6in) diameter, including 5mm (¼in) seam allowance.

One circle of fabric for the back 14.5cm (5¾in) diameter, including 5mm (¼in) seam allowance.

Two circles of muslin 14cm (5½in) diamater, including 1cm (⅜in) seam allowance.

65cm (25in) crossway strip 2.5cm (1in) wide.

1.20m (1⅜yd) lace 2cm (⅞in) wide.

Lavender.

Preparation

1 Cut 18cm (7in) from the crossway strip and make a length of rouleau (*see figure 174*).

2 Join the two circles of muslin together on the seam line using a small straight machine-stitch, leaving a 5cm (2in) gap in the seam. Turn right side out through the gap in the stitching.

3 Through the gap fill the muslin bag with lavender.

4 Oversew the gap keeping the stitches small and close.

Making up

1 Centre the muslin bag on the wrong side of the back.

2 Cover the muslin bag and back with the patched motif right side up.

3 Tack together the back and the patched motif, encasing the muslin bag, on the seam line, easing the motif to fit and allowing it to dome.

4 Fold the prepared length of rouleau in half to form a loop. Place at top centre back with the raw edges together. Tack.

5 Bind the outer edge using a zipper presser foot for the machining.

6 Gather the lower edge of the lace to fit the hemmed edge of the binding on the back of the bag. Pin in place. Hem.

7 Remove all pins and tacking.

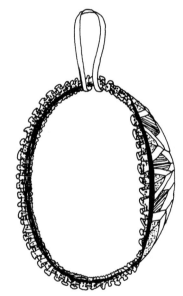

159   Sketch of lavender bag

158   Lavender bag worked in printed polyester and cotton lawn, velvet and satin

6 Useful processes and stitches

In previous chapters references have been made to processes and stitches which are explained below. Some additional processes have been included that are particularly useful when completing articles that are decorated with mitred patchwork.

Left-handers should work hand-made stitches in the reverse direction to the diagrams. If the diagram is held in front of a mirror the reflection will be in reverse.

SEAMS

Bonded open seam

When fabric in the seam is very bulky it is inclined to rise and not stay flat. This can be overcome by bonding the seam allowance in place. When the seam allowance is turned back the long stitches holding the patches in place are inclined to slacken; the bonding has the second advantage that it prevents this slackening taking place.

Method

1 Put right sides together and pin or tack in place.
2 Stitch on the seam line (*figure 160a*).
3 Remove pins and tacking.
4 Press the seam open and flat.
5 Insert strips of Bondaweb between the seam allowances and the wrong side of the garment (*figure 160b*).
6 Bond in place according to the manufacturer's instructions.

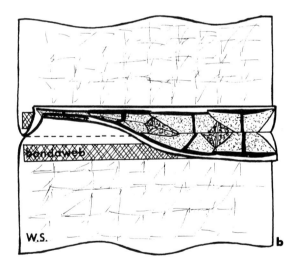

160 Bonded open seam
    a Stitching the seam
    b Bonding the seam allowance

Laid seam

Where a patched fabric is joined to an unpatched fabric a laid seam is used.

Method
1 Put right sides together and pin or tack in place.
2 Stitch on the seam line. Remove pins or tacking.
3 Press the seam allowances towards the unpatched fabric (*figure 161*).

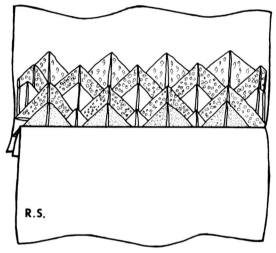

161 Laid seam

Top-stitched seam and insertions

As well as holding the fabric in place, top-stitching emphasises a seam line.

Method
1 Press the seam allowance on the unpatched fabric to the wrong side. When a motif is inserted within the fabric, first stitch very near to the seam line in the seam allowance. This is known as stay stitching. Snip any inward curves or corners up to the stay stitching then press the seam allowance to the wrong side (*figure 162a*).
2 Tack the unpatched fabric in place over the patching, having the folded edge on the seam line.
3 Machine stitch close to the folded edge using a slightly larger stitch length than normal.

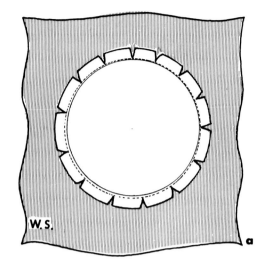

162 Insertion of a motif
   a Inward curve stay-stitched and snipped; seam allowance turned to wrong side
   b Motif top-stitched in place

4 Remove the tacking (*figure 162b*).

Slip stitch

Although not very strong, slip stitch is a most useful method of joining together two folded edges invisibly from the right side of the work.

Method
1 Put the folded edges together.
2 Make a stitch about 3mm ($\frac{1}{8}$in) long in the fold of one edge.
3 Exactly opposite where the thread emerges

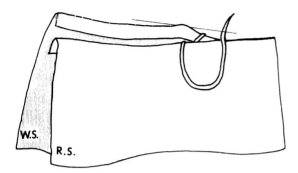

163 Slip stitch: joining two folded edges together

insert the needle in the fold and make a stitch about 3mm ($\frac{1}{8}$in) long.

4 Repeat steps 2 and 3 to the end of the seam, making a small tug on the thread after each stitch to draw the folded edges together (*figure 163*).

Joining crossway strips

Crossway strips cut from oddments of fabrics are often too short in length and require a number to be joined together. The join must be made on the grain of the fabric.

Method
1 Having cut out strips of fabric the required width and on the true bias, cut the ends to be joined on the straight of grain (*figure 164a*).
2 Put right sides together with the acute angles extending. The more they extend, the larger the seam allowance will be.

3 Stitch parallel to the raw edges from one right angle to the other (*figure 164b*).
4 Press the seam open and flat.
5 Trim away the extending acute angles of fabric (*figure 164c*).

EDGINGS

Binding an edge

Binding is a useful method of neatening edges. It is particularly useful when many layers of fabric must be joined together, and eliminates turnings that would be very bulky at the edge of an article. Crossway strips, purchased bias binding, braid, tape or ribbon can be used to form the binding.

Method for crossway strips
1 Cut crossway strip for the binding. The strip can be cut from fabric that matches or contrasts in colour to the article and is suitable for its use. The width of the crossway strip should be twice as wide as the required finished edge plus two seam allowances. If necessary, join strips to make the required length.
2 Pin the crossway strip to the article with right

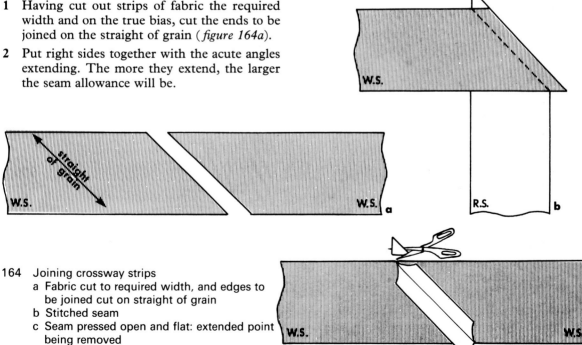

164 Joining crossway strips
  a Fabric cut to required width, and edges to be joined cut on straight of grain
  b Stitched seam
  c Seam pressed open and flat: extended point being removed

sides together and the seam lines matching. Slightly stretch the strip on inward curves and ease on outward curves. The centre along the length of the strip must fold at the finished edge of the article. If the beginning and end of the binding meet, join them together on the straight of grain. Make this join at a seam position or centre back of the article. If ends finish at a neatened edge, fold over a small turning to the wrong side. Tack in place. Remove pins.

3   Stitch together on the seam line.

4   If necessary trim away any excess seam allowance from the article.

5   Fold the crossway strip over the edge of the article.

6   Turn under the raw edge of the strip and hem to the line of machine stitches.

Method for purchased bias binding
When using purchased bias binding, open out one of the folded edges and place the crease mark on the seam line of the article with right sides together. Proceed as for crossway strips. The second folded edge of the bias binding should lie along the line of stitching for hemming in place. The article seam allowance may need to be trimmed but take care that the patching stitches are not cut.

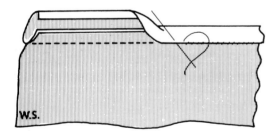

165   Binding with crossway strip or bias binding

Method for braid, tape or ribbon
Braids which are diagonally woven can be used for straight or curved edges. Tape or ribbon can only be used on straight edges as they do not stretch or ease into place.

1   Fold and press the braid, tape or ribbon along the length so that the under-section is 2mm ($\frac{1}{16}$in) wider than the upper section (*figure 166a*).

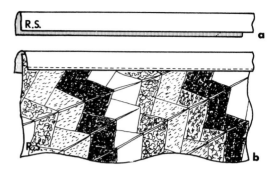

166   Binding with braid, tape or ribbon
   a Folding braid, tape or ribbon
   b Binding stitched in place

2   Place the binding over the raw edge of the article having the wider part on the wrong side of the article. Tack in place making sure the stitches pass through both edges of the binding.

3   Machine all layers together, having the stitching close to the edge of the upper section of the braid, tape or ribbon (*figure 166b*).

Method for backing fabric
To reduce the bulk when applying mitred patchwork motifs to garments or articles, the backing fabric on which the motif has been made can be turned onto the right side to form a binding. The backing fabric would either be reversible or the patching must be completed on the wrong side of the fabric.

1   Cut the backing fabric with an allowance around the motif that is the depth of the binding required plus 4mm ($\frac{3}{16}$in).

2   Press 4mm ($\frac{3}{16}$in) towards the patches.

3   Fold over the remaining fabric onto the patches and tack in place (*figure 167a*).

4   Position the motif on the article and tack in place.

5   Machine near the hem edge of the binding. Remove tacking (*figure 167b*). The outer edge may also be stitched down if required. An alternative to using two rows of straight stitching is zig-zag stitch. The motifs on the caftan in figure 127 were applied using this alternative.

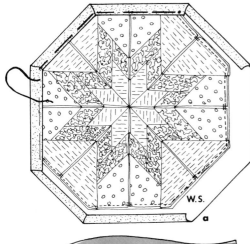

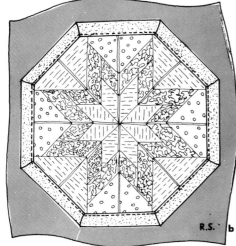

167 Backing fabric binding and appliqué
    a Patched motif with backing fabric binding the straight edges
    b Bound motif applied to right side of article fabric

Hem with mitred corners

This is an attractive and neat method of making a hem and reducing fabric bulk at corners. It is used for the border round the cot quilt shown in figure 142. The hem may be turned onto the right or wrong side of an article. For this reason the diagrams in figure 168 are shaded but not labelled with right and wrong sides.

Method

1 Mark the fold lines of the hem and turnings by pressing or with tacking (*figure 168a*).

2 Make a crease mark across the corner as shown in figure 168b, being careful not to stretch the fabric.

3 Fold the fabric diagonally. If the hem is to be on the right side of the article, place wrong sides together; if the hem is to be on the wrong side of the article, place right sides together (*figure 168c*).

4 Machine or hand back-stitch on the creased line, stopping at the marked turning fold line. Cut off excess fabric.

5 Press the seam open and flat (*figure 168d*).

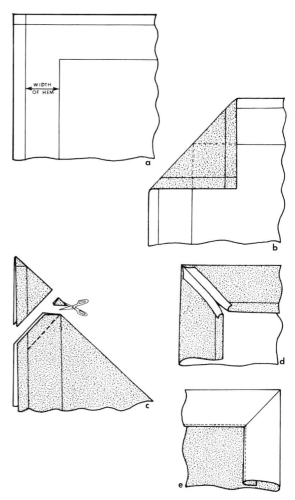

168 Hem with mitred corner
    a Marked fold lines of hem and turnings
    b Marking crease-line across corner
    c Stitched seam and excess fabric removed
    d Seam pressed open and flat
    e Hem stitched in place

6 Turn the hem inside out.

7 Turn under the raw edge to the marked turning fold line (*figure 168e*).

8 Stitch the hem in place with a suitable method for the article.

Saw-tooth edging

This is an attractive edging that complements mitred patchwork.

Method
1 Cut out a number of squares of fabric. An average size is 5cm (2in) but they can be any size, depending on the appearance required.

2 Fold diagonally (*figure 169a*).

3 Make a second diagonal fold (*figure 169b*).

4 Slot one triangle inside another and tack together near the raw edges (*figure 169c*).

5 Place the triangles onto the right side of the article with all raw edges together.

6 Place the lining or facing on top with the right sides facing and raw edges together.

7 Stitch on the seam line.

8 Turn the lining or facing to the wrong side and press (*figure 169d*).

Prairie points

Prairie points are another attractive edging that complements mitred patchwork. They can be made from squares of fabric folded as for saw-toothed edging, or folded in a mitre as for mitred patchwork, or made from stitched equilateral triangles of fabric.

Method using squares of fabric
1 Cut out 5cm (2in) squares of fabric. Smaller or larger squares may be used according to the effect required.

2 Fold as for saw-toothed edge or for mitred patchwork.

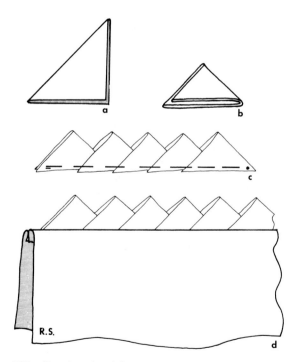

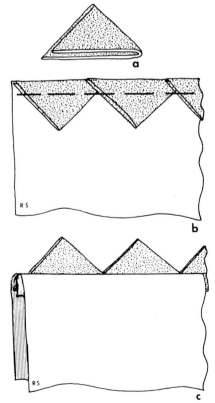

169 Saw-tooth edging
   a Square of fabric folded diagonally
   b Second diagonal fold
   c Triangles slotted together and tacked
   d Edging inserted into seam

170 Prairie points using folded patches
   a Folded square
   b Patches tacked in place for edging
   c Edging completed

3 Tack the triangles onto the right side of the article, having raw edges together and overlapping the triangles so that they cross exactly on the seam line. The mitred patches have the mitred side facing the right side of the article (*figures 170b and 171b*).

4 Pin or tack the lining or facing on top with right sides together and raw edges together.

5 Stitch on the seam line.

6 Remove pins and tacking.

7 Turn the lining or facing to the wrong side and press (*figures 170c and 171c*).

Method using stitched triangles

1 Cut out equilateral triangles.

2 Put two triangles right sides together.

3 Stitch on the seam line along two edges.

4 Trim away top point (*figure 172a*).

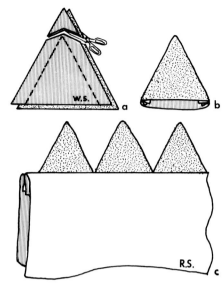

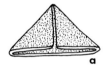

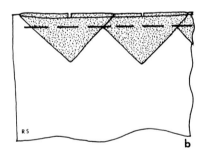

171 Prairie points using mitred patches
  a Mitred square
  b Patches tacked in place for edging
  c Edging completed

172 Stitched triangle edging
  a Stitching preparation of triangle
  b Turned triangle
  c Triangles inserted into a seam

5 Turn right side out (*figure 172b*).

6 Stitch into the edge of the article as for folded or mitred prairie points (*figure 172c*).

Piped edging

Piped edging can be used to decorate or emphasise an edge. The piping is made from crossway strips and is inserted into the edge in the same way as prairie points. The crossway strip may have a piping cord encased inside, but the cord should be pre-shrunk before insertion and a zipper presser foot is necessary when machining so that the stitching is close to the cord (*figure 173*).

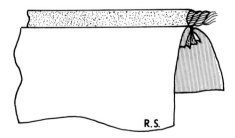

173 A piped edging

Rouleau

This is a narrow tube of fabric made from a crossway strip. It is useful for ties and loops used as fastenings. As the same fabric used in an article can be used to make the rouleau, any fastenings can match perfectly and become an integral part of the article. Crossway strips used for binding an edge can extend to become a rouleau to form a tie or loop without the necessity of stitching additional ties onto the article.

Method

1 Cut crossway strips twice the finished width plus two seam allowances. The seam allowances should be just a little less than the finished width.

2 Fold the strip in half along the length with right sides together.

3 Stitch on the seam line. Do not trim the seam allowances as these form the filling in the tube.

4 Firmly attach a strong thread to one end at the seam line.

5 Pass the thread down the tube using a bodkin or a thick blunt needle, inserting the eye first (*figure 174a*).

6 Pull the end of the tube through until the right side is outside (*figure 174b*).

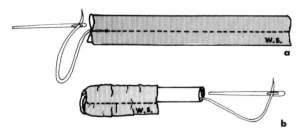

174 Making a rouleau
a Crossway strip stitched to make a tube and ready to turn right side out
b Rouleau tube being turned right side out

STITCHES

Herringbone stitch

Herringbone stitch is a most useful handworked stitch as it is broad and flat. It can be used for holding down and covering raw edges as well as being a decorative embroidery stitch. See figure 175 for the two stages of working.

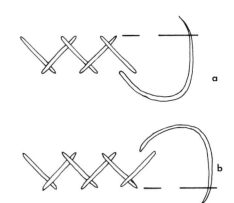

175 Herringbone stitch
a Upper stitch being made with thread below the needle
b Lower stitch being made with thread above the needle

Spider web, woven and stem stitched wheels

Webs and wheels are handworked embroidery stitches that form a solid circle. They are made over a foundation of straight stitches and are more easily worked by using both a sharp-pointed needle (crewel) and a blunt-pointed needle (tapestry).

Method for woven wheel

1 Using a crewel needle, make a foundation of an uneven number of straight stitches to form a circle. Insert the needle near or at the centre of the circle.

2 Bring the thread up to the right side between two of the straight stitches and near the centre of the circle (*figure 176a*).

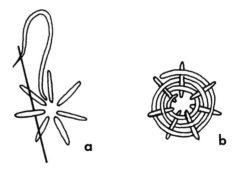

176 Woven wheel
a Prepared odd number of straight stitches, the needle passing under the stitches not through the fabric
b Completed woven wheel

3 Change from the crewel needle to a tapestry needle. Weave under and over the foundation stitches until the circle is filled (*figure 176b*).

4 Take the thread to the back of the work and cast off.

Method for spider web

1 Using a crewel needle, make a foundation of any number of evenly spaced straight stitches to form a circle. An even number of stitches can be made either across the diameter or to the centre of the circle.

2 Bring the thread up to the right side between two straight stitches near the centre of the circle.

3 Change from the crewel needle to a tapestry needle. Working on the foundation stitches only, make a back stitch by passing the thread back over one straight stitch then taking the needle forward under two straight stitches. The needle should always be on the outside of the thread (*figure 177a*).

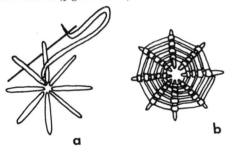

177 Spider web
  a Prepared straight stitches, the needle making a back stitch passing under the stitches not through the fabric
  b Completed spider web

4 Repeat, working continuously round until the circle is filled (*figure 177b*). The foundation stitches will be encircled by the thread forming raised spokes.

5 Take the thread to the back of the work and cast off.

Method for stem stitch wheel

1 Using a crewel needle, make a foundation of any number of evenly spaced straight stitches to form a circle. Even numbers of stitches can be made either across the diameter or to the centre of the circle.

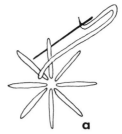

178 Stem stitch wheel
  a Prepared straight stitches and needle making a stem stitch passing under the stitch and not through the fabric
  b Completed stem stitch wheel

2 Bring the thread up to the right side between two of the straight stitches and near the centre of the circle.

3 Change from the crewel needle to a tapestry needle. Working on the foundation stitches only, make a stem stitch by passing the thread forward over two straight stitches and the needle back under the second straight stitch. The needle should always be on the outside of the thread (*figure 178a*).

4 Repeat, working continuously round until all the circle is filled (*figure 178b*).

5 Take the thread to the back of the work and cast off.

French knot

This is a very useful stitch to make a single textured dot; many packed close together make a mass of texture.

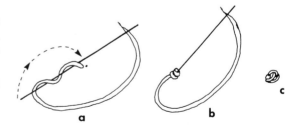

179 Making a French knot
  a Twist thread round the needle then turn the needle in direction of arrow
  b Needle inserted into fabric and thread tightened
  c Completed knot

Method

1 Bring the thread to the right side of the fabric in the position for the knot.

2 Wrap the thread anticlockwise twice round the needle (*figure 179a*).

3 Turn the needle clockwise and insert into the fabric very near to the position where the thread emerged (*figure 179b*).

4 Tighten the thread round the needle.

5 Pull the needle through to the wrong side (*figure 179c*).

Whipping back

Whipping back is a method of casting off machine thread ends by hand to prevent the machining becoming unstitched.

Method

1 When commencing and finishing a row of machining, leave long thread ends.

2 Pull the upper thread through to the wrong side of the work.

3 Thread both the upper and lower threads into a tapestry needle (blunt point).

4 Stitch over five machine stitches, passing the needle under each stitch without picking up any fabric (*figure 180*).

5 Cut off thread ends close to machine stitches.

Tailor tacks

Tailor tacks are an excellent method of temporarily marking fabrics on both the right and wrong sides of fabric. The tacks are easily removed without leaving any marks when the work is completed.

Method

1 Thread a needle with a long length of double thread. A darning cotton or an embroidery thread are suitable because they do not slip easily out of fabrics.

2 Take a stitch at the point to be marked, picking up the pattern paper and all the layers of fabric requiring marking. Do not use a knot at the end of the thread but leave a long tail hanging.

3 Make a second stitch in the same place and through all layers. Do not pull the thread tight but leave a loop. The more layers of fabric being marked the larger must be the loop and tails.

4 Cut off thread leaving a long tail (*figure 181a*).

5 Cut the loop in the centre.

6 Carefully remove the pattern, pulling the threads through the paper.

7 Ease the layers of the fabric apart.

8 Cut the threads between the fabric layers leaving tufts of thread marking the positions on each piece of fabric (*figure 181b*).

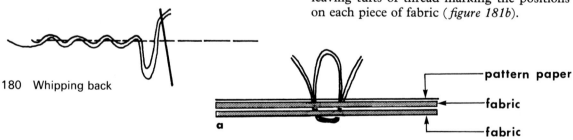

180   Whipping back

pattern paper
fabric
fabric

a

181   Tailor tack
  a Tailor tack made through
    paper pattern and
    two layers of fabric
  b Tailor tack cut through
    loop and paper
    pattern removed;
    threads cut between
    separated fabrics

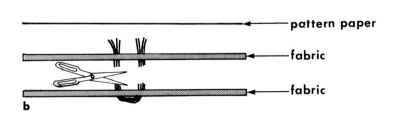

pattern paper
fabric
fabric

b

MOUNTING

Samples of work always look more attractive if the raw edges are concealed and the work is set into a neat window. The mounted samples can be labelled with relevant information and filed together for future reference. A good-quality mounting card, white or a suitable colour, should be used.

Method

1 Carefully mark the window position on the right side of the card using a sharp H pencil. Make the window smaller than the sample to conceal the raw edges. Straight lines are easier to cut than curves but the window need not always be a rectangle.

2 Using a metal rule and a sharp pointed craft knife, score the card on the marked lines, being careful not to extend beyond the corners. Have the rule on the frame side of the marked lines not the window side (*figure 182*).

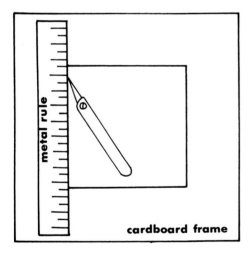

182 Cutting a cardboard frame for mounting

3 Make a number of scores until the knife penetrates the card. Never use force when scoring. It is better to make many scores rather than pressing heavily, otherwise the card will not cut cleanly.

4 Remove the loose card from the window. Sometimes the corners are obstinate. Use the point of the knife and score away from the corner in both directions until the card lifts away. This will ensure neat precise corners.

5 On the wrong side of the card frame spread some latex adhesive near, but not at, the window edges.

6 Place the frame on top of the sample, being careful to position accurately.

7 Press down firmly, then allow the adhesive to set before proceeding further.

8 Cut a piece of backing paper the same size as the mounting card; cartridge paper is very suitable. Record on this paper any information you need for future reference, e.g. types of fabrics and thread, supplier's name and address, any special problems you had during the making of the motif.

9 On the back of the mounting card spread a line of latex adhesive up to the outer edges, taking care not to allow any glue onto the front. Although latex adhesive can be rubbed off, some coloured cards will be spoiled if the adhesive spreads onto the right side.

10 Place the backing paper onto the wrong side of the mounting card. Press down firmly along the glued edges. Allow the adhesive to set.

If you wish, title or label the front of the mounting card. Dry transfer lettering is very useful for this as it gives a professional finish. Dry transfer lettering is made more permanent and less likely to peel off during use if it is sprayed with a fixative.

BIBLIOGRAPHY

America's Quilts and Coverlets Carleton L. Safford and Robert Bishop (E. P. Dutton & Co. 1975)

Adventures in Patchwork Dorothea Nield (Mills & Boon 1975)

Embroidery Volume 33 No. 3 Autumn 1982

Patches Old and New Agnes M Miall (Woman's Magazine Office 1937)

Popular Crafts November 1982

Quilters' Guild Newsletter No. 1 Winter 1979 No. 9 Winter 1981

Quilting with Folded Star Craft Course Publication (California 1981)

SUPPLIERS

Great Britain

John Lewis & Company Ltd, Oxford Street, London W1A 1EX, for a wide selection of fabrics, craft materials and haberdashery.

McCulloch & Wallis Ltd, 25–26 Dering Street, London W1R 0BH, for a wide selection of fabrics, and all sewing materials and accessories.

Mace and Nairn, 89 Crane Street, Salisbury, Wiltshire, for frames, embroidery fabrics and threads, and sewing accessories.

Limericks, Hamlet Court Road, Westcliff-on-Sea, Essex, for sheeting in white and many colours.

D. G. Chatfield, 41 Ecton Lane, Sywell, Northampton, for mail order service of ready mitred mouldings and sundries for picture framing.

Milner Leather, Cilycwm, Llandovery, Dyfed SA20 0SS, for all types of leather in small pieces or skins.

USA

Mail order suppliers

American Handicrafts, 2617 W Seventh Street, Fort Worth Texas 76707, for all craft supplies.

The Counting House at the Hammock Shop, Box 155, Pawleys Island, So Carolina 29585, for materials, threads, hoops, needles and frames.

Economy Handicrafts, 50–21, 69th Street, Woodside, New York 11377, for all craft supplies.

Lee Wards, Elgin, Illinois 60120, for all craft supplies.

Peter Valley Craftsmen, Layton, New Jersey 07851, for all craft supplies.

The Stearns & Foster Co., P.O. Box 15380, Cincinnati, Ohio 45215, for batting and frames.

Vermont County Stores, Weston, Vermont 05161, for calico prints.

Chain stores

Ben Franklin Stores	Neishers
Jefferson Stores	J. C. Penney Stores
Kay Mart	Sears Roebuck
M. H. Lamston	Two Guys
The May Co.	Woolco

Index